TOP GUN

TOP GUN

The Navy's Fighter Weapons School

Text and Photographs by George Hall

Presidio Press ★ Novato, California
THE PRESIDIO POWER SERIES
AIRPOWER #1007

Library of Congress Cataloging-in-Publication Data

Hall, George (George N.)
  Top Gun, the Navy's Fighter Weapons School.

  (The Presidio Power Series; Airpower #1007)
  1. Navy Fighter Weapons School (U.S.) 2. Fighter
plane combat—United States. I. Title. II. Series.
VG94.5.S3H35 1987   358.4′14′071173   86-30479
ISBN 0-89141-261-1

All photographs copyright © George Hall 1987, with the exception of:

  p 5, 50: Lt. Dave Baranek USN

  p 12-13, 18-19, 21, 22, 26, 77: US Navy via Robert Lawson/ Tailhook Photo Service

  p 33, 35: Robert Lawson/Tailhook Photo Service

  p 42-43: Grumman Aerospace

  p 51: General Dynamics

  p 78-9: Matt and Mark Waki

  p 107: Juha Karkkainen Lehtikuva/Woodfin Camp Inc.

Author photo credit: Roger Ressmeyer

Printed and bound in Korea.

Contents

Acknowledgements

A person writing about Top Gun runs into the same problem that surprises a lot of Top Gun students: you might think you know the story, but there's far more to it than you could have imagined. I had a great deal to learn in a short time, but like the Top Gun students themselves, I had some superb instructors.

The Top Gun staffers know their material cold, and all hands were extremely helpful and forthcoming—at least with the aspects of the curriculum that aren't classified. To all those who helped, my thanks: you know who you are. Herewith a special mention to a few who went the extra mile: Executive Officer Tom "Sobs" Sobieck, Lt. Comdr. Bob "Rat" Willard, Lt. Comdr. Pete "Horse" Caulk, Lt. Dave "Bio" Baranek, and Lt. Linda "Snail" Speed. I also got a world of great information and anecdotes from a trio of former Top Gun teachers: Comdr. John Ed "Tiger" Kerr, Comdr. C. J. "Heater" Heatley, and Lt. Col. Manfred "Fokker" Rietsch, U.S.M.C.

Telling any story about the modern military means starting with the Public Affairs shop. As with a number of projects in the past, we enjoyed terrific support and cooperation from Comdr. Tom Jurkowsky and the all-knowing Senior Chief Fred Larson at COMNAVAIRPAC, NAS North Island. Equally helpful, and a lot of fun, were Lt. John "Smegs" Semcken and his right hand Mitzi Conaway at NAS Miramar.

I owe special appreciation to Don Simpson, Jerry Bruckheimer, and Tony Scott, producers and director of Paramount's sensational *Top Gun*, for allowing me to tag along during the filming of the movie at NAS Miramar and NAS Fallon, Nevada. I was able to photograph magnificently choreographed dogfights that would have been virtually impossible to put together in real life.

And if by chance there are still a few readers who haven't caught the film, run, don't walk, to the nearest Bijou.

Air-to-air shots were taken from the affable Clay Lacy's "Astrovision" Learjet, and during flights in a Top Gun F-5F with either Lt. Greg "Hollywood" Dishart or Lt. Sandy "Jaws" Winnefeld in the front seat. Special thanks to these superb pilots for the ultimate inequity: suffering in polite silence while I took over and tried (unsuccessfully) to keep us from getting creamed by a couple of smart-ass F-14 students.

Additional shots were taken with radio-controlled cameras mounted in a cylindrical pod hanging from an underwing weapons pylon. The large picture on the front cover is an example.

For my history of air combat and for my explanations of the various formations, techniques, and maneuvers, I have cadged mightily from two excellent texts, *Fighter Combat* (Naval Institute Press, 1985) by Navy (and now Air Force Reserve) fighter pilot Bob Shaw and *Fighter Pilot Tactics* (Stein and Day, 1983) by the prolific Mike Spick.

Finally, blame me rather than any of my sources if I've gotten anything wrong. Responsibility for the accuracy of what you're about to read rests solely with your faithful scribe.

George Hall

Previous spread: Tomcats of VF-302 "Stallions" lift off from NAS Miramar.
Facing page: Top Gun plane captain gives the age-old high sign prior to taxi.

Origins

San Diego is a wonderful city, blessed with spectacular beaches, California's best weather, and a laid-back atmosphere that makes it feel like a much smaller town. San Diego and the U.S. Navy go way back together; a Pacific base since the late nineteenth century, the city currently plays host to three aircraft carriers, more than one hundred surface ships, several major headquarters, an immense supply apparatus, scores of blue-water defense contractors, and thousands of Navy retirees who knew a good thing when they first saw it.

Naval aviation has had roots in San Diego from its first moments; the Navy's first aviator, one Lt. T. G. Ellison, took his flight training from the Army at Camp Glenn Curtis in 1911 and established an official Navy presence on the Coronado peninsula a year later.

Naval Air Station North Island, a small field only a mile across San Diego Bay from the downtown, hosts carrier-borne S-3 Viking antisub units, a number of helicopter outfits, and a steady stream of admin traffic related to the various headquarters and to the carriers operating in the Pacific practice areas to the southwest. Take the Cabrillo Freeway ten miles north and you'll be in the middle of NAS Miramar, a gigantic base that shrieks with naval air activity almost twenty-four hours a day. We'll check in at the main gate for a look around. Be forewarned: in these days of heightened security, the Marine Corps guards check every car and require a call from an on-base sponsor before admitting any nonmilitary visitor.

Miramar calls itself "Fightertown U.S.A.," and with good reason. Almost half of the Navy's F-14 Tomcat fighters are based here, more than 150 of the huge $30 million machines. Eight Tomcat squadrons are arrayed along the flight line.

Several units will be deployed on carriers at any given time, occasionally for at-sea periods approaching one year. But the outfits left behind keep the base humming. Midfield is VF-124, a Replacement Air Group, or RAG, for training new Tomcat drivers and back-seat Radar Intercept Officers. On the far right are the Navy's first Reserve F-14 squadrons, VF-301 and -302, both loaded with high-time veterans of air combat in Vietnam. Nestled between are Miramar's other prime operational tenants, several squadrons of E-2C Hawkeye early-warning aircraft.

The Miramar pattern is seldom silent. Tomcats blast down the twin runways in full afterburner, a spectacle hard to ignore. Hawkeyes, handsome twin-engine turboprops with slowly rotating twenty-four-foot radomes, shoot precision touch-and-go landings. And two thousand feet up, a perfect fingertip formation of F-14s screams down the runway center line, Blue Angels–close at four hundred knots, for the "break," the classic military traffic entry; each bird snaps into a five-G turn, seconds apart, transonic vapor streaming above the wing roots, airspeed bleeding as the huge variable-geometry wings sweep forward, rolling out smoothly for the anticlimax of the downwind leg. Flightline crews have stood and worked under thousands of these breathtaking arrivals, but few can avoid at least a moment's glance upward. It's the exquisite essence of modern military aviation.

Previous spread: F-4 Phantoms of the Marine Reserve VMFA-112 "Cowboys" cavort off the north coast of Molokai, Hawaii.
Facing page: The Navy's premier fighter base, NAS Miramar, plays host to half the F-14 Tomcat squadrons as well as Top Gun, the Navy Fighter Weapons School.

3

Now another pair of Tomcats roars into the break, each trailing on its outer wingtip a tiny fighter half its size. Back on the ground and clear of the active runway, the two small ships, one an A-4, the other an F-5, taxi in echelon to the far south end of the flightline. Unlike the ghost-grey Tomcats, these fighters sport mottled camouflage schemes—green-brown on the A-4, blue-grey on the F-5. Foot-high aircraft numbers, piped in the manner of the Soviet air force, are painted on their noses. The fighters park amidst a dozen of their number on the apron beside Hangar One, home of the Navy Fighter Weapons School. The NFWS is known universally by its nickname: Top Gun.

The immense F-14A Tomcat, designed as a long-range fleet defense interceptor, is an astonishingly good dogfighter in capable hands. Large "glove" containing mechanism for variable-sweep wings adds greatly to aircraft's total wing area.

Top Gun is a graduate course in fighter weapons and tactics for Fleet and Marine Corps fighter aircrews. The standard course, running five weeks and given five times a year, is designed to bring in the best crews in each fighter aircraft community and make them a quantum leap better. Squadron skippers in the F-14, the F/A-18, and (for a short while longer) the F-4 outfits are asked to pick their best crews and send them to Miramar with their aircraft for, in the words of one student,

"the best month of flying in a naval aviator's career." These crews will then return to their units as repositories of the latest and hottest gouge on enemy threats, tactical developments, and ragged edge-of-the-envelope flying in their particular aircraft. A couple from each class might even be asked to join the best of the best of the best — the Top Gun instructor staff.

Top Gun was a direct outgrowth of Navy pilots' experiences in the Vietnam war. These experiences, up to the bombing halt in 1968, were less than terrific. Navy fighter pilots had posted kill ratios as high as 15:1 against Japanese pilots in the Pacific war; Air Force Sabre jocks manhandled Communist MiG-15s in Korea by margins of between 7:1 and 14:1, depending on whose figures you believe. America's tactical air performance in Vietnam was dismal by comparison, with 2.5:1 at best, even dropping *below* 1:1 in some particularly disastrous 1968 engagements. Something was desperately amiss — the United States was fielding first-class aircraft, including the awesome F-4 Phantom and the immensely capable F-8 Crusader, whereas the North Vietnamese relied heavily on a twenty-year-old design, the subsonic MiG-17, plus a smattering of supersonic but indifferent MiG-21s. American pilot training had always been second to none. But somewhere along the line some crucial lessons had been forgotten. Answers had to be found — no country, not even the United States, could long afford to trade Phantoms and precious two-man crews for Gomer Frescoes and Fishbeds.

In 1968 the Naval Air Systems Command told an experienced Navy fighter and attack jock, Capt. Frank Ault, to find some answers and report back. The now-famous "Ault Report" pulled no punches. Three principal areas of concern were called out. First, the wondrous air-to-air missiles which were to bring an end to messy, close-in dogfighting were a catastrophic disappointment — the expensive radar-guided AIM-7 Sparrow boasted less than one kill for every ten shots, and the heat-seeking Sidewinder, while faring somewhat better, was still a heartbreaker. Second, the bitterly resented rules of engagement, supposedly necessitated by the politics of the war, gave limitless advantage to the enemy. And third, Ault called for more realistic air combat training, preferably against dissimilar aircraft types flying a simulation of enemy tactics.

Ault's particular suggestion was for a fighter pilot's graduate school, a "Ph.D." program in weapons usage and air combat maneuvering (ACM). A class for Navy F-4 crews was begun in March of 1969, and Top Gun was established as an independent command three years later. Trained crews returned to fleet squadrons, passing along their newfound knowledge to squadron mates and providing some show and tell in the skies over Route Pack 6. Kill ratios shot up dramatically, rising to 12:1 in 1972. Air Force ratios remained relatively unchanged; they lagged in realistic training efforts until after the end of the war. Comdr. Randy "Duke" Cunningham, naval aviation's leading Vietnam ace with five MiG kills, was a graduate of the first Phantom class; he recalls translating his Top Gun lessons directly into combat victories.

The original Top Gun has evolved into a whole curriculum of air combat courses. The school's intense teaching schedule is built around the so-called Power Projection course; this is the Top Gun familiar to moviegoers, and it is the school's primary reason for existence. Twelve fighter crews — two-man F-4 and F-14 teams, plus F-18 pilots — gather at Miramar for an ultra-intense, five-week course featuring some thirty ACM hops, daily classroom instruction, and one-to-one sessions with Top Gun teachers. Navy adversary pilots, who emulate enemy fighter tactics in the A-4, F-5, T-38 and F-21 Kfir aircraft, are also run

Top Gun Skyhawk trails the two principal student-flown aircraft, the F/A-18 Hornet (*foreground*) and the F-14 Tomcat.

through the first two-thirds of the Power Projection class. These professional Gomers are usually experienced and accomplished ACM drivers, having been trained in their Adversary and Composite squadrons. Combat air controllers, who guide intercepts from ships, ground stations, and E-2 Hawkeye radar aircraft, are also included in the entire course of instruction.

In addition, Top Gun offers a refresher course for newly minted squadron commanding and executive officers, for carrier air group commanders (CAGs), and for the occasional flag rank. The one-week FAST (Fleet Air Superiority Training) class is given to air wing elements responsible for Fleet air defense, usually the two F-14 squadrons plus their companion E-2 Hawkeye

The F/A-18 Hornet offers a matchless combination of tight-turning ability with tremendous energy in either horizontal or vertical planes. Here the bird honks into a 7-G turn with afterburners blazing.

unit. As the Navy's new F/A-18s are increasingly involved in the outer air battle, they will also join in FAST training. The new OAST (Overland Air Superiority Training) course is taught and flown over barren desert ranges out of NAS Fallon, Nevada; a team of several Top Gun staffers takes a few jets and a lot of research out into the weeds for this one-week combination of lectures and strike-oriented hops. Attack and early-warning assets are also brought into the OAST exercises.

As if the schedule at Miramar isn't hectic enough, small groups of Top Gun pilots and RIOs (Radio Intercept Officers) hit the road in their F-5s and A-4s to bring their brand of ACM instruction directly to the Fleet and Marine Corps fighter outfits around the country. Detachments to Europe and the Far East, although not common, are occasionally authorized, with the Top Gun birds being left at home. Individual Top Gun pilots and RIOs are often detailed to guest tours with the Air Force Aggressors and the Fighter Weapons School, both at Nellis AFB near Las Vegas.

In between the various courses, there are the normal administrative duties, certifications, periodic check rides and other details that are a necessary part of any military flying outfit. The school's high profile, particularly since the 1986 release of Paramount's hugely successful movie, requires the staff to host and brief a steady stream of Washington politicians, foreign generals, and fascinated journalists looking for an elusive new angle on the Navy's top pilots.

And then there is the lecture. Each Top Gun instructor is required to master a particular subject and conduct a class on this subject for each group of Power Projection students. Whatever his subject—forward-quarter missile attack/defense, one-versus-one dogfighting (1V1), the changing Soviet threat, techniques for teaching and learning—the Top Gun teacher is expected to prepare himself to the point where he knows literally as much about his topic as anyone on the planet. After months of research and organization, the instructor will present his lecture to small groups of his colleagues for fine tuning and criticism. When he feels he is ready, he will subject himself to a "murder board"—a formal presentation before the assembled Top Gun faculty.

They don't call it murder for nothing. These sessions frequently eat up an entire workday, as the man of the hour expounds on his subject, fields complex questions, and generally dodges flak, friendly and otherwise. The result is a perfectly honed hour or two of sophisticated instruction and a teacher who will feel sublimely confident presenting his topic to any audience at any time. But it's a lot of work and not much fun. Any Top Gun jock would sooner launch solo into a skyful of pissed-off MiGs than relive his murder board.

Despite the killing pace and the constant shortage of hours in the day, Top Gun is a dream assignment for any naval aviator. Lt. Col. Manfred "Fokker" Rietsch, Top Gun's first Marine Corps instructor and a continuing legend around Miramar, remembers, "Sure, it was a hell of a lot of work, but the flying! Two or three hops every day, sometimes more, nothing but all-out ACM against really top-notch guys. We just can't do that in the squadron; there are so many other tickets to punch. I learned a lot, taught a lot, flew my butt off, and had a great time. It doesn't get better than that."

A History of Air Combat

The French, as usual, have a saying: "The more things change, the more they stay the same." Nowhere is this aphorism more apt than in the realm of air combat. Despite unimaginable advances in aircraft, weaponry, communications, and control, a surprising number of basic dogfighting rules have remained valid since their formulation over the trenches of France.

It was, in fact, a Frenchman who got the whole thing started. In the early months of World War I, both French and Germans put airplanes into the airspace of the other, primarily to reconnoiter and shoot reconnaissance photos. On 5 October 1914, a French Voisin biplane came upon a German Aviatik, its crew paying them little attention as they studied the French lines below. Back-seater Louis Quenault, firing a ring-mounted machine gun, mortally damaged the German craft. It was history's first air-to-air kill.

Both sides took to air combat, and in only a few months the British, French and Germans were all flying dedicated fighter aircraft — craft whose mission was not to photograph, not to spot for artillery units, not to harass ground forces, but to attack and destroy other airplanes in flight. In mid-1915 the Germans unveiled their revolutionary Fokker Eindecker (monoplane); it was pathetically underpowered, as were all World War I aircraft, but it was agile, durable, and an excellent climber. The Eindecker was fitted with a forward-firing machine gun synchronized to avoid hitting the two-blade propeller; it can be argued that serious air-to-air combat began with this seminal invention. When flown by such superb German pilot-tacticians as Max Immelmann and Oswald Boelke, the Eindecker was utterly deadly.

Immelmann and Boelke were amazingly advanced dogfighters for their day. The original Immelmann turn was the forerunner of today's vertical tactics; after gaining height behind his prey, Immelmann would swoop down, fire a burst through the pullout, then use his momentum to gain as much as a thousand feet in a vertical climb (aircraft of the time were scarcely able to manage a normal climb rate of three hundred feet per minute as a rule). As his craft lost energy at the top of the zoom, he would hammerhead or stall-turn and plummet into another slashing attack. (The term "Immelmann" in modern acrobatic flying has taken on an entirely different meaning. It now refers to a climbing half-loop with a 180-degree roll at the vertical to allow the craft to complete the loop upright.)

The father of World War I air combat was Oswald Boelke. A teacher before the war, he wrote a manifesto of air combat principles in 1916 which remain astonishingly apt today. The Boelke dicta:

1. Secure all possible advantage before attacking. Gain position, strength of numbers, surprise; use the sun, the clouds, height, speed.

2. If you initiate an attack, carry it through. Aggressiveness and determination are critical attributes in a fighter pilot. Break off too early and you'll simply encourage and embolden your opponent.

3. Fire only at close range. Less important in the days of air-to-air missiles, of course, and yet gun attacks are far from dead. The low-velocity guns of Boelke's day required all manner of deflection, trajectory, and Kentucky windage skills to make long-range hits in a turning fight. These problems could be bypassed, suggested Boelke, by simply closing to a range where they didn't matter—like twenty meters, Boelke's preferred shooting distance!

4. Keep your eye on your opponent. Even in the present era of radar and supersonic speeds, there is no substitute for eyeballing the bad guy. You'll see it posted all over at Top Gun: "Lose sight, lose the fight."

5. Attack your opponent from behind. Still the best policy, even with the development of all-aspect missiles. You hold all the cards when you're on the adversary's six; you have time for a good shot, you're in position to follow through with guns if your missile attack should fail, and best of all, he can't shoot back. Just don't forget about his wingman.

6. If an opponent dives to attack you, turn and meet him. If you question this rule, simply reread number 5 above. Head at him, and he'll enjoy only a fleeting shot. And you'll have your opponent in front of your own three-nine line, the all-important imaginary line through your wings. You can't kill anyone who's behind your three-nine line, but he can sure as hell kill you.

7. Always remember your line of retreat. This isn't a simple matter of reading the compass; it also means remaining aware of your fuel state, the possibility of enemy forces getting between you and home, and other factors. Over North Vietnam, a long, skinny, vertical country, fighter and attack aircraft tried to set up for west-to-east passes; if they took a hit, they stood a much better chance of making it to the sea.

8. Fly and fight in groups of four to six. Should the fight break down into a series of single combats, try to keep several of your aircraft from attacking a single opponent. Among many other innovations, Boelke is credited with the idea of the wingman, who can watch your tail while you attack. He went on to develop section and division tactics as World War I battles evolved with ever-larger numbers of aircraft.

Boelke formed his own hand-picked fighter squadron, Jagdstaffel 2. All of his pilots were drilled in his methods; they even studied the capabilities of, and flew against, captured enemy aircraft! Boelke met an uncharacteristic end—in a furball with two British DH2s, he collided with his wingman as both tried to gain a shot opportunity. The master died ignoring the last of his own rules.

Midway through the first world war, multi-plane tactics took on new sophistication and depth as large numbers of aircraft clashed over France. The British employed multi-level formations of twelve aircraft, with three four-plane sections separated by as much as two miles and three thousand vertical feet. Leaders usually stayed low, with the other aircraft arrayed upwards and outwards, as visibility in biplanes was best forward and down. Instructions were relayed by hand signal and colored flares fired from Very pistols. Likewise the German "flying circuses" flew as highly trained units, generally at the direction of a supremely skilled and charismatic leader. But efforts to maintain strict formation control usually degenerated when the battle was joined.

Despite this trend toward division tactics, many of the war's highest-scoring aces, such as

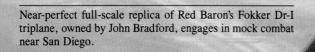

Near-perfect full-scale replica of Red Baron's Fokker Dr-I triplane, owned by John Bradford, engages in mock combat near San Diego.

Manfred von Richtofen and England's James Mc-Cudden, preferred solitary one-versus-one combats. Both pilots were cautious fighters, patient stalkers, and matchless aerial marksmen; each had a cold-blooded preference for the more gratuitous kills—preoccupied photo-recon planes, injured stragglers, obvious novices. Von Richtofen once estimated that four-fifths of his victims never detected his deadly presence until it was too late. This is another of the eternal rules of fighter combat; the 80 percent estimate has remained a good rule of thumb from the Red Baron's day to the stunning Israeli successes over Lebanon's Bekaa Valley. The element of surprise remains the fighter pilot's greatest ally.

Aerial hostilities resumed in the midthirties over two widely separated venues, Spain and China. In a prelude to World War II, Germany, Italy, the Soviet Union and Japan jumped at these chances to test and practice their newest weapons and tactics in the air as well as on the ground.

By 1936 fighter and attack aircraft bore little resemblance to the underpowered wood-and-fabric crates of the first world war. Metal monoplanes such as the Messerschmitt Me-109, the Japanese Type 95, and the Russian Polikarpov I16 could fly three times as fast and climb ten times as fast as World War I fighters. Armaments included large numbers of heavy machine guns (eight in the British Hawker Hurricane) and even rapid-fire cannon. More significantly, fighting aircraft now routinely carried two-way voice radio; pilots could talk to each other, and they could be controlled and vectored to the fight from the ground.

Nazi Messerschmitt pilots perfected loose wing formations over Spain; the "pair of pairs," or *schwarm*, became the standard for most fighters in World War II, allowing for excellent cover and resistance to the surprise bounce. The squirrelly, hard-to-maneuver Polikarpovs developed vertical dive-and-zoom tactics as a counter to the superior horizontal or turning capabilities of their Italian and German adversaries. In China the highly trained Japanese utterly overwhelmed their Chinese and Soviet opponents. Participation in these parochial conflicts gave Axis military units a tremendous leap forward in real combat experience. English and American fighter pilots were forced to learn the perilous ropes almost overnight in the Battle of Britain and the onset of war in the Pacific.

Much has been written on the epic British defensive air battles; no complete exposition will be attempted here. The skill, courage, and achievements of England's fighter pilots in this arena remain the stuff of legend, and when Churchill spoke of so much being owed by so many to so few, he was speaking of these men. But the key element in this victory was Britain's rudimentary early warning system, a low-tech but workable radar net that permitted placement of defensive fighter formations at the right point in space and time. Although London and the southeast ports suffered horribly in the bombardments, the German aerial offensive ultimately failed, and the Luftwaffe never completely recovered from the loss of hundreds of its most experienced fighter and attack pilots.

British Hurricane and Spitfire pilots were gunning primarily for Nazi bombers; strenuous attempts were made to avoid dogfighting with German escorts. Not surprisingly, the Luftwaffe Messerschmitt drivers would have none of this. Close escorts and high-cover fighter formations covered the bombers like a cloud and attacked the Brits ferociously. The Royal Air Force countered

by splitting its fighter missions, with the Spitfires as a rule going air to air with the Me-109Es and the heavier eight-gun Hurricanes hitting the Nazi bombers.

Speeds had increased enormously since the biplanes had tangled over the Western Front. Head-on closure at a distance of two miles had dropped from half a minute to less than ten seconds. RAF attackers took delight in manic head-on gun passes at the German bombers; the crews of the latter viewed the world through a huge all-Plexiglas nose, and the psychological effect of the head-to-head attack could terrorize and scatter even veteran bomber pilots.

The advent of unimaginably massive Allied bombing raids over Germany handed a number of defensive advantages over to the Luftwaffe. Defending one's own soil, of course, has a way of focusing and distilling one's skills. The poor range of the Me-109E, which gave it such short turn-and-burn times over England, ceased to be a problem; now it was the Allied fighter escorts that had to fight with one eye on the fuel gauge. And in 1942 the Germans fielded hundreds of the new Focke Wulfe 190, a small, simple fighter with the best performance statistics in the European skies. England countered with a much improved Mark IX Spitfire. Dogfighting speeds, G-loads, and general ferocity increased apace.

American P-51 Mustangs were soon accompanying the bombers, slinging long-range drop tanks which allowed them to go the distance while fighting on the way in and out. The Mustang could hold its own with the best that the enemy could put in the air. Surprisingly the P-47 Thunderbolt, a low-level attack craft known universally as the "Jug" because of its barrel-chested profile, performed admirably as a bomber escort. Its ability

to climb and turn was limited, but its weight and horsepower enabled it to bounce Nazi fighters with fearsome, high-speed dive and zoom tactics. The American bombers, performing one of the most difficult and tragically bloody missions in the whole history of military aviation, had to rely on huddled formations and massed defensive firepower for their salvation. It is said that throughout all aerial warfare four out of five victims did not detect their assailants until too late. The European daylight bomber forces were the painful exception to that dictum; the crews almost always saw their attackers but could do painfully little to protect themselves.

America's Pacific war had of course begun with the disciplined and devastating Japanese attack on Pearl Harbor. Navy and Marine Corps pilots encountered a well trained and combat-experienced carrier fighter force, mounted primarily in the Mitsubishi A6 M2—the Zero. This outstanding little fighter, with its light wing loading and excellent power-to-weight ratio, could fly rings around the F4F Wildcat, America's first-line carrier fighter. The American pilots, shaken by early encounters with the Zero, quickly developed aggressive teamwork and maneuvers to counter the few weak spots in the Zero's makeup.

Above all, the Zero had poor survivability; fuel tanks were not self-sealing, and the pilot's position was unarmored. If the clumsy Wildcat could get its sights on the Japanese fighter, its .50-cal guns

would almost invariably be deadly. Among the most lasting maneuvers developed during the early war years was the "Thach Weave," named after its inventor, VF 3 skipper Lt. Comdr. John Thach. This was a beam defense tactic; two pairs of Wildcats would fly line abreast some four hundred yards apart. If either side was bounced, the pairs would turn hard toward each other. A Zero pilot who pressed his attack would find himself face to face with the other two Wildcats and twelve blazing wing guns. After the pass the American fighters would complete the scissors and resume the line-abreast spread with positions reversed. Thus teamwork, aggressiveness, and morale, coupled with the amazing ability of the "Grumman Iron Works" Wildcat to sustain battle damage, allowed the Navy to meet and defeat the hot little Japanese fighter.

The battles of Midway, Guadalcanal, and the Marianas decimated the ranks of experienced Japanese combat pilots as America's pilot pool grew correspondingly stronger and more canny. New Navy and Marine fighters—the F6F Hellcat and the F4U Corsair—could do a much better job of fighting both vertically and horizontally with the Zero, especially at higher altitudes. Terrible attrition left the Japanese military virtually bereft of aircraft and pilots by the end of the war.

Scarcely five years after the end of World War II, American fighter pilots found themselves tussling in a new transonic arena over the Korean

North American FJ-3D Fury was navalized version of Air Force F-86 Sabre during and after the Korean War. As a rule, Navy fighters concentrated on ground attack rather than ACM in the Korean conflict.

border with China. Although Navy and Marine Corps carrier pilots flew attack missions in the Korean War, the vast majority of air combat was between the U.S. Air Force's F-86 Sabres and Soviet-built MiG-15s, the latter flown by Russians as well as Chinese and North Korean pilots. The venue was "MiG Alley," an imaginary triangle bordering Manchuria on the Yalu River. Industrial targets in this triangle were subjected to aerial attack by United Nations forces, with the Sabres flying "CAP" (combat air patrol) to fend off the MiGs. Clashes in the alley often involved more than a hundred jets.

The Communists held the cards in MiG alley. Their airfields were just across the river, while the Sabres had to fly two hundred miles into a fierce 100 MPH jetstream. A state-of-the-art radar system gave the Communists ample warning; the MiGs could marshal and gain altitude over China, jumping into battle with the advantage of height. Worst of all, the rules of engagement put Manchuria off-limits to U.N. pilots, while the MiGs could flee across the river whenever things got too rough.

And then there was one more ace: the MiG-15 itself. This light, tough fighter was superior in almost every way to the F-86—speed, turning ability, rate of climb, vertical energy. It carried 23mm and 37mm cannon, while the Sabre had only a sextet of .50-cal machine guns, indifferent armament even by World War II standards.

Yet the MiG Alley air battles led to the loss of 750 MiGs versus one hundred F-86s, a highly respectable ratio by any reckoning. Pilot training, initiative, and morale clearly spelled the difference. Great stress was placed on the leader-wingman pair, with new pilots being given six days of in-country instruction in two-plane sec-

tion tactics and general balls-to-the-wall air combat maneuvering. Aggressiveness, skill, and attitude carried the day. Here is yet another eternal truth of air combat; in von Richtofen's words, "The quality of the crate matters little. Success depends on the man who sits in it."

Vietnam found American pilots relearning old ACM lessons at great cost. Air Force, Navy, and Marine fighter jocks flew an awesome new craft, the twenty-five-ton, two-engine, two-seat F-4 Phantom. The Phantom, with its King Kong radar and air-to-air missiles, would certainly change the nature of the air battle; the close-in knife fight of old would give way to radar intercepts and beyond-visual-range attacks with the AIM-7 Sparrow, an unbeatable new radar-guided missile. Gomers who somehow got past the Sparrows could be readily dispatched with the short-range AIM-9 Sidewinder, a nasty little heat-seeker that would literally fly up the enemy's white-hot tailpipe. The age of infallible push-button air combat had arrived, and incomparable American technology would rule the skies. Guns were eliminated from most Phantoms in cavalier fashion; what use could they serve in the air wars of the sixties?

The results over North Vietnam were nothing short of disastrous. Everything went wrong. The complex Sparrows almost never worked; at one point U.S. fighters fired *fifty-five* of the costly hummers without a single score. Even worse, two

American aircraft were hit at maximum range by Sparrows, prompting new rules of engagement that insisted upon firm visual identification before shooting. So much for the long-range intercept. The gunless Phantoms found themselves dogfighting after all; the bad guys flew small, hard-to-spot MiG-17s and MiG-21s, while the immense Phantoms with their smoky engines could be seen forever. Eighteen Air Force fighters were lost to MiGs in the last half of 1967 for the loss of only five of the enemy.

Some agonized rethinking was clearly in order. Politics halted all air fighting over the North in March of 1968, and the hiatus lasted until 1972. The Navy took advantage of the stand-down to analyze their experiences and figure out some new moves. Top Gun was born during this period; the first class of F-4 crews reported to NAS Miramar in March 1969. This nucleus of trained ACM experts would return to the fleet and impart their findings to the others in the squadron. Borrowed A-4 Skyhawks and Air Force T-38 trainers would be used to simulate, in size and performance, the MiG-17 and MiG-21 respectively. Subsequently the Northrop F-5, a single-seat fighter with a strong visual similarity to the T-38, would take over the supersonic MiG-21 role.

When aerial warfare resumed over the North in 1972, a different story unfolded. Navy Phantom and Crusader (a hot, gun-toting carrier fighter with a single engine and a single seat) pilots were ready to party with the little enemy jets. Newly developed vertical tactics successfully nullified the superior turning abilities of the MiGs; the Sparrows were still heartbreakers, but the infrared Sidewinders had been tweaked to much greater reliability. Navy kill ratios shot from dismal parity before the bombing halt to 12:1 by the

Now in its third decade of Navy and Marine service, the enormously capable F-4 Phantom is nearing the end of its active duty. This Marine Rhino is attached to the only remaining RAG, VMFAT-101 at MCAS Yuma, Arizona.

25

end of the conflict. Today visitors climbing the stairway, or "ladder," to the Top Gun offices are treated to an awesome display—scores of red silhouettes on the white wall, each signifying a MiG kill (plus a hapless pair of Libyan Sukhoi Fitters) by a Top Gun–trained crew.

Air warfare in the eighties has continued to demonstrate the applicability of the age-old rules. Superb training, an aggressive spirit, and the mind-boggling trickery of the vertical-takeoff Harrier helped a small British Navy/RAF contingent thrash the competent and courageous Argentines in the South Atlantic. The Argie Skyhawk and Mirage pilots faced an insurmountable

difficulty; the Falklands were at the absolute limit of their combat range, leaving them all but unable to engage in any fuel-burning ACM with the ferocious Brits. The French Mirage III, an asskicking Mach-2 fighter, was thus held to subsonic speeds by its inability to use even a few seconds of gas-guzzling afterburner. In addition, the Argentines were clearly psyched by the unusual flying capabilities of the Harrier. Vectoring its rotary thrust nozzles in flight allows the little jet to tighten its horizontal turn unnaturally. Even more

Many Navy fighter jocks still fondly consider the gun-bearing F-8 Crusader, shown here over the Gulf of Tonkin in 1971, as the "tits machine" of all time. French Navy pilots still operate the Crusader on their carriers.

astounding is its ability to decelerate by rotating the nozzles *forward*; the Harrier can drop 200 MPH worth of airspeed in seconds without climbing, and no conventional fighter on its six o'clock can avoid a potentially fatal overshoot. The Harrier jock can then slam the nozzles aft, all the while maintaining full thrust, and accelerate like something out of *Star Wars*. Although designed as a unique low-level attack craft, the Harrier in British and U.S. Marine Corps hands has been developed into an amazingly capable dogfighter as well.

In 1982 the superb Israeli Air Force put it all together in an epic air battle with the Soviet-supplied Syrians over Lebanon's Bekaa Valley. Boelke's first rule of air combat has never been more effectively employed. The IAF dealt itself every card: matchless pilot training, two of the world's finest fighters (American-built F-15s and F-16s), Sparrows that finally hit what they went after, the new all-aspect Lima version of the venerable Sidewinder (which also performed perfectly on the Falklands Harriers), and all manner of electronic trickery—airborne early warning, radar jamming, tiny drones that catalogued the locations of the surface-to-air missile sites. The Syrian MiG-21s and MiG-23s were utterly overwhelmed, many of them taking max-range Sparrow hits only seconds after lifting from their runways. Completely demoralized and panicked, whatever determination and aggressiveness the Syrians possessed had evaporated by the third day of fighting. The score was probably the most lopsided in the history of air combat: Israel over Syria, 82-zip.

History shows us that equipment is important, but only to a point. Pilot skill, aggressiveness, and teamwork will carry the day in almost every

imaginable instance. Luftwaffe ace Adolph Galland's words, emblazoned artistically in Top Gun's library, summarize it best:

Only the spirit of attack borne of a brave heart will bring success to any fighter aircraft, no matter how highly developed it may be.

Top Gun teachers Greg "Hollywood" Dishart and Dave "Bio" Baranek talk close-in tactics on Hangar One's ladder. Silhouettes of MiG-17s and MiG-21s symbolize actual Navy/Marine kills in Vietnam.

The Learning Curve

The Navy and Marine aviators who train and teach at Top Gun regard themselves as the finest military pilots on earth. They may very well be right. Standing atop a pyramid of accomplishment unlike that of any other flier, they share ample reason for their seemingly egotistical pride and attitude.

Navy pilots are a self-selecting lot; it's not a vocation a person pursues casually or accidentally. Virtually all are college graduates. Those who haven't followed a Navy ROTC or service academy program to an officer's commission will first attend a twelve-week Aviation Officer Candidate School of the sort made famous in the film *An Officer and a Gentleman*. Regardless of background and education, the aviator-to-be is clearly of a type; he's motivated, mature, a self-starter, a good (although usually not blindingly brilliant) student, a guy (or girl) who has managed effortlessly to mix academics, extracurricular activities, competitive athletics, fun with the opposite sex, and steering clear of serious trouble. It is frequently pointed out, although statistics are elusive, that Navy and Marine pilots are often first or only sons.

A quick word about women flying in the Navy. The Navy does train female pilots, although not many—less than 5 percent of the total. Federal law dictates that females in the military cannot hold down combat slots in any branch of the service; hence women pilots in the Navy (there are none in Marine Corps aviation) tend to fly support and patrol craft, multi-engine heavies like the P-3, the C-130, and the C-9, C-1 and C-2 COD (Carrier On-Board Delivery) birds, and some helicopters, or "helos" in universal Navy parlance. A tiny handful have entered the jet pipeline to emerge as pilots of A-4 and A-7 attack craft in training, composite or test squadrons, where they instruct, tow targets, and even fly a bit of adversary ACM. The best of these women jet jocks, like Lt. Chrys Lewis and Lt. Beth Hubert, garner the highest marks from fellow male aviators who've seen them in action, and a day may well come when they'll wind up in combat cockpits. In the meantime, however, we'll stick hereinafter to the male pronoun in writing the Top Gun story.

While we're at it, a bit of information about the Marines. The U.S. Marine Corps has its own self-contained air arm, flying a mix of combat aircraft such as the F/A-18 Hornet, the vertical-takeoff Harrier, the F-4 and RF-4 Phantom, the A-4M and A-6E attack jets, the EA-6B ELINT bird, and an assortment of transports and helos. The Marines, though they hate to discuss it, are an adjunct of the Navy, and all of their aircrews are Navy trained. Marine F-18 and F-4 crews attend Top Gun routinely, and they're known to kick their share of ass since they get a lot of solid ACM practice in their squadrons. In addition, several Jarheads are always in attendance on the Top Gun instructor staff. So when I talk of Navy pilots in the remainder of the book, I'm talking about the Marines as well.

The newly minted Navy ensign or Marine Corps second lieutenant, once given the nod for flight training, heads for the cradle of naval aviation, NAS Pensacola, Florida, for indoctrination

---

Previous spread: "Hollywood" Dishart awaits start-up in two-seat Top Gun F-5F. Your intrepid author is playing RIO in the back seat.

and primary flight training. A superb bill of health, including perfect 20-20 nonastigmatic eyesight, is a prerequisite for pilot training. Applicants with everything but the eyes are split off into NFO (Naval Flight Officer) training, from which they will emerge as potential F-14 and F-4 backseaters, A-6 bombardier/navigators, E-2 airborne combat controllers, or electronics systems wizards in S-3 antisub or EA-6B radar-jamming birds.

At Pensacola the student spends some eleven weeks actually learning to fly, ultimately soloing and logging time in the T-34, a single-engine turboprop trainer. Washouts are not uncommon, but about 70 percent come out the other end to face the first big cut, the three "pipelines." It's a tough time. Most hotshots want jets, but the Navy operates lots of helos and multi-engine airplanes. It's an understatement to say that not everyone

Marine Phantom lights the fire prior to ACM engagement at NAS Dallas, Texas. The Navy is now out of the F-4 business altogether, but Marine squadrons will operate the huge fighter-bombers for several more years.

comes away happy, and it's widely known that one's chance of weaseling into jets after training and seat time in something else is minimal.

The three pipelines are called "Maritime" (thirty-eight weeks leading to checkout in the P-3, the C-130, the C-9, or the E-2 Hawkeye), "Helo" (forty weeks for SH-3, LAMPS, Huey, or CH-53 heavies), and the fervently desired nirvana, "Jets." The latter takes some forty-eight weeks, half of it basic training in the fat and forgiving T-2 Buckeye, half advanced work in the TA-4 Skyhawk.

The lucky jet selectee finds himself being fitted for a set of exotic "speed jeans," a nylon G-suit that, when connected to the jet's bleed-air system, will automatically inflate to squeeze his legs and abdomen under G-loadings, thus minimizing the pooling of blood in the lower extremities. Then it's off to a shit-hot year in jetland, at bases in Texas, Mississippi, or good old Pensacola.

The first jet hops come only a couple of weeks later. The fat little Buckeye is no cold-steel exotic, but it *is* a jet, and the student finds himself forced

Sunset catapult shot of a Navy F/A-18 Hornet from the USS *Constellation* somewhere in the western Pacific.

Lexington cat officer genuflects in the traditional "shoot" signal as a student readies himself for his first solo catapult shot. Aircraft is T-2 Buckeye primary jet trainer.

to keep ahead of an airplane that flies three times as fast as the primary T-34. He also finds himself inching toward the naval aviator's ultimate rite of passage – banging a screaming jet down onto a rolling steel carrier deck at some 150 MPH. Instructors in the T-34 emphasized smooth touchdowns preceded by a gentle, nose-high flare; the back-seater in the Buck is now urging the student to slam the jet down in a violent collision with the runway, following the elusive movements of a Fresnel light landing aid similar to the all-important "ball" on the port side of the carrier deck.

After a bunch of practice carrier approaches on a land-bound runway, the student goes "feet wet" with his T-2 and lines up on the training carrier USS *Lexington*. He'll bag his first four "traps," or arrested landings, each followed by a short taxi to the catapult and a mind-stopping "cat shot" that will propel the trainer from zero to 160 MPH in under two seconds. Our boy is a tailhooker now, and the rest of his time in the Buck – instrument work, formation flying, some basic fighter maneuvers and gunnery — will streak by in a blur.

The student now has a firm grasp of the basics of military jet flight. What follows is twenty-four weeks of advanced work in the Skyhawk, a hot and feisty attack jet similar to those flown by the Top Gun instructors and (until early 1987) the Blue Angels. It gets deadly serious now, with low-altitude, high-speed navigation exercises, lots of ACM, the ever-present instrument work, and more traps aboard the *Lexington*, this time in a jet far less forgiving than the Buckeye. Eighteen months and three hundred air hours after coming through the Pensacola gate, a new jet jock is awarded his Wings of Gold.

Pipeline time again. The student's performance and preferences, plus the Navy's needs, are correlated by computer, and the student is given "the word on the bird" — F-14 Tomcat, F/A-18 Hornet, A-6 or A-7 attack jets, the antisub S-3 Viking, the EA-6B Prowler, the T-39 or C-21 (Learjet) executive transports. Again some will be disappointed, but ultimately every Navy pilot will end up defending his bird against all detractors. Fighters? Kings of the sky. Attack? We do the real damage to the enemy — the fighters just cover for us. Antisub? The most desperate threat to the carrier will come not from the air but from beneath the sea. AWACS? Tankers? Transports? Linchpins all, the battle is hopeless without us. Search and rescue? Just wait until you're dodging bad guys in some Godforsaken jungle after taking a hit and punching out. The beauty is that all are correct. Each mission is critical, and each requires the best the Navy can find.

But whatever the reality, the fighter boys place themselves at the very tip of the pyramid; an inordinate number of first choices are for Tomcats

and Hornets. Performance as a student counts for a great deal — eagerness and bold aggressiveness in ACM, going for it in formation flying (frequently terrifying the first few tries), mastery of the all-important carrier landings, complete command of instrument "headwork," a general confidence, but not cockiness, around the jet. There's also a sizeable element of luck in the process. Put bluntly, your class might graduate at a time when there are a lot of fighter openings, and it might not. Pilots remember whole classes being steered into, say, A-7s, or large groups of basic students being sent to fill gaps in helo or multi-engine communities, regardless of their potential as jet pilots.

New fighter pilots report to RAGs (Replacement Air Groups) on either coast for yet another year of learning to fly either the F-14 or F-18 (in the rarified fighter world the dual-role Hornet is never referred to by its official "F/A-18" designation, and fighter jocks suppress involuntary shudders at the mere thought of rearranging the earth's surface by the undignified dropping of explosive ordnance). Pilots "CarQual" with a requisite number of day and night traps aboard an active-service carrier off San Diego, Jacksonville, or Norfolk; they learn the tricky task of in-flight refueling, fly lots of instruments, and above all they learn to employ their jets' exotic weapons systems. Next comes the real thing, reporting in at a Fleet or Marine squadron with over 450 hours

Section of student-flown Buckeyes enters the break over the training carrier *Lexington* prior to arrested landings.

Landing Signal Officers, here fielding an A-7 Corsair II, control and grade every carrier trap.

of total flight time in the log. The U.S. Navy will have spent more than a million dollars training this new hotshot; it will now hand him the keys to an aircraft worth anywhere from $20 million for the F-18 to over $30 million for the Tomcat. Exotic ELINT rigs like the early-warning E-2C Hawkeye or the radar-jamming EA-6B Prowler have price tags that are hard to pin down, but they start at $60 million and wander upwards.

Somewhere between advanced jet training and the RAG, most Navy pilots are christened with an unofficial nickname, or "call sign." Like it or not,

Facing page: The night carrier landing is the naval aviator's ultimate rite of passage; all do it routinely, but it is the rare pilot who claims to enjoy it. Here a Hornet gropes toward the darkened ramp of the *Constellation*.

it will probably stick with its owner for an entire career. In tactical radio conversations, the pilots and RIOs will use these shorthand monickers in lieu of aircraft numbers or flight names. Hence no one is ever nicknamed "Sam," or a wingman asking Sam to break right would occasion a skyful of six-G bat turns as entire strike packages pushed on the pole to avoid surface-to-air missiles.

The call sign is a cherished badge of arrival in naval aviation. It usually refers to physical appearance or an event in training better forgotten; it might be a play on the pilot's name. A guy named Campbell is likely to become "Soup," and any Ward will get "Psycho." You get the idea. Efforts to anoint oneself with a call sign seldom stick. Young Lt. Randy Cunningham successfully switched himself from "Yankee" to "Duke"— he was and is a diehard John Wayne fan—and the change was tolerated because he was on the fast track to becoming the Navy's first Vietnam ace. Some Norfolk F-14 boys remember a recent arrival, fresh from the RAG, who called himself "Lightning." He had a way of bugging senior pilots, telling them things they already knew about the airplane, and he was a bit bug-eyed to boot. So "Lightning" quickly became "Bug," and Bug he'll be forever, like it or not.

My favorite call sign tale is about one of the first women to make it through the Navy's jet pipeline, Mary Lou Jorgensen, now a shit-hot A-4 pilot with experience in training and test squadrons. The boys saw her coming and tagged her "Jugs" in honor of her spectacular superstructure. Feminists would no doubt be horrified, but they'd be missing the exquisite point. Far from being sexist, her call sign is a badge of acceptance—magnificently embarrassing, tasteless, and *right*. It marks Jugs as, well, one of the boys.

The mystique of the naval aviator is inextricably linked with the carrier landing; it is the essence of his knighthood, the feat that sets him apart from all other pilots. Approaching the boat (to aviators it's always "the boat," a cheerful insult calculated to enrage the surface types who run the carrier for them) on a clear, calm day is an eye-opener. Regardless of aircraft type, the pilot is aiming his arresting hook at a rectangle only forty feet deep—the size of a big living room. In that rectangle are four 1½-inch steel cables; snaring one will bring thirty tons of airplane to a stop in a couple of hundred feet. Although there are four cables, the pilot is ideally going for the #3 wire,

and each landing in his career is graded by Landing Signal Officers, so the pressure is unrelenting. Of course, there is far more than a grade at stake. Coming in low might result in a "ramp strike," which is every bit as bad as it sounds; survival of plane and crew will be problematical. A high pass will lead to a "bolter," or go-around. All carrier aircraft go to full military power upon touchdown so that if they miss the wires they'll be able to thunder back into the pattern for another try.

It's plenty tough on a nice day, but the whole game changes radically at night. Visual cues are almost nonexistent, the deck remaining tactically unlit except for pinprick lights along the edges. Religious faith in the instruments is the pilot's only hope since massive vertigo can engulf the pilot who relies too much on his eyes and inner ear sensors. A Fleet pilot will be expected to make about a third of his carrier landings at night. The stress of the night landing is unimaginable. More than a few carrier pilots have come aboard on black, stormy nights, climbed from the cockpit, walked into the skipper's office, and laid their treasured wings on his desk. A monstrous dread has overwhelmed them. A person can get killed doing this for a living.

Navy pilots love their work—they're shit-hot and they know it. But it's simply not possible to find a carrier aviator who looks forward to night traps. Add in a few other little distractions— driving rain, gusting wind, a roll or pitch to the invisible deck—and the task strains the limits of human capability. Yet it is expected that the pilots will successfully bring their aircraft aboard. It is without question the most difficult *routine* feat in all aviation. Navy pilots know that it is their peculiar and magnificent badge of honor.

Back to Top Gun. The altar boy good looks of

Tom Cruise might give the impression that Top Gun students are fresh out of a college fraternity, but in fact their average age is closer to thirty. The Top Gun–chosen aren't new to fighters; most will have at least five hundred hours in type on their log books and at least one six-month sea cruise as well. Fleet and Marine fighter squadrons are periodically invited to send pilots and RIOs to the Power Projection course. They might be chosen unilaterally by the squadron skipper, or some sort of unit fly-off might be set up with a Top Gun stint as first and only prize.

The students fly to Miramar in a squadron bird, and a small maintenance detachment comes along to keep the plane on line. There has been some thought given to providing Top Gun with a line-up of its own Hornets and Tomcats, in the manner of the Air Force's Fighter Weapons School at Nellis AFB, but no concrete action so far. The idea has merit, as the squadrons are taxed somewhat by putting one of their best jets out of service for six weeks. It comes down to money priorities, and Top Gun isn't holding its collective breath.

Top Gun is all about air-to-air combat, and at present it is largely limited to instruction in only two modern fighters, the F-14 Tomcat and the F-18 Hornet. The noble F-4 Phantom, the aircraft around which Top Gun was originally created, will soon be but a memory in the Navy and Ma-

Top Gun students roll their Tomcats into the break for landing at Miramar. The variable-geometry wings are motoring forward into landing configuration.

rine Corps. The Marines operate the only remaining F-4 RAG at MCAS Yuma, Arizona, and it will close up shop in 1987. Even the Navy Reserve is giving up on "Old Double-Ugly," with the two squadrons at NAS Dallas gearing up for conversion to the Tomcat even as we speak. There remain shit-hot Phantom drivers who can fight the big bird with the best of the vaunted fourth generation, but the plane is *old*, hard to maintain, and it just doesn't, well, *fit in* any more. Still, there's not a more soul-stirring sight in all military aviation than a "Rhino" blasting down the runway at dusk in full burner. There is slight solace—we'll probably see Phantom variants in limited military service until the end of this century, in photo-recon and "Wild Weasel" (surface-to-air missile suppression) missions. Long live the magnificent Rhino.

The F-14 Tomcat is the follow-on to the Navy Phantom, and it now makes up about two-thirds of every Top Gun Power Projection class. The Navy operates some twenty F-14 squadrons, plus a training RAG on each coast, with more than three hundred aircraft in all. About forty Tomcat crews can expect to attend Top Gun each year.

The Tomcat is a huge aircraft, bigger and heavier than medium bombers of World War II, capable of being catapulted from a carrier at gross weights exceeding thirty-two tons. Being big, of course, is no advantage in air combat, and no free world fighter is bigger. The Tomcat was not conceived as a dogfighter: echoing the experience with the Phantom, it was designed to be an immensely capable fleet defense interceptor. It's probably fair to say that its architects at Grumman never envisioned it going to school at Top Gun.

The F-14 is probably the only dual-crew fighter around that doesn't have a secondary ground-attack mission. The back-seat Radar Intercept Officer is in charge of the Tomcat's fighting heart, the AWG-9 Doppler radar and weapons system. The aircraft was literally built around this system and its long arm, the AIM-54 Phoenix air-to-air missile. The Phoenix is currently the most sophisticated and complex missile in the air. It is huge (over 1,000 pounds), hyper-fast (Mach 4-plus), and it can reach out one hundred miles from the Tomcat under electronic guidance from its parent fighter, the E-2 Hawkeye, and its own internal gadgetry. The AWG-9 system can track and classify twenty-four separate aerial targets, launching up to six Phoenixes at the most serious threats. Live firings have been limited, due to the extremely high cost of the missile, but accuracy in all Phoenix shots to date has exceeded 90 percent. "Six crazed little Kamikaze wingmen hanging under your butt," Top Gun XO and back-seater Tom "Sobs" Sobieck fondly calls them.

Fortunately the F-14's designers didn't saddle the Tomcat crew with a single attack option. The plane can (and in combat situations always does) carry a mix of AIM-7 Sparrow and AIM-9 Sidewinder missiles, the latter having an all-aspect attack capability in the Lima and Mike variants. And, shades of the F-8 Crusader, the gun is back—to wit, the six-barrel M-61 20mm rotary cannon. In the F-14's only real dogfight to date, a section from the VF-41 "Black Aces" fired one AIM-9L Sidewinder each to blast a pair of Libyan

Right: The classic Phantom will soon be a memory in naval aviation, but it's hard to imagine a more dramatic sight than a Rhino leaning on the loud pedal as it blasts off into a Pacific sunset.

SU-22 "Fitters" into the Gulf of Sidra in 1982. Each 'Winder was let loose at a range of less than a mile, and each Tomcat was poised to finish things off with the gun if the missiles failed to track.

Despite its size, the F-14 is an amazingly agile and nasty dogfighter in capable hands. Its thrust-to-weight ratio is good, especially at lighter load-outs, and its wing loading (pounds of gross weight per square foot of wing area) is surprisingly light, especially when its variable-geometry wings are racked fully forward. In addition, a glance at the Tomcat's vertical planform (see page 6) reveals a gigantic aerodynamic wing root, or "glove," which effectively increases usable wing area by at least a third. All this wing flapping in the breeze lets the Turkey "bat-turn" with much smaller fighters, frequently to their astonishment. Adversaries trying to go horizontal with the Tomcat learn to watch for telltale signs of the Big Move: burners lighting up, the huge jet rolling into a pure vertical bank, and those enormous wings motoring forward.

In spite of its proven abilities, the F-14 is actually underpowered. Its Pratt & Whitney TF-30 turbofans, with about 20,000 pounds of thrust apiece, aren't quite up to the job; in addition they've been inexcusably troublesome and failure-prone. A dismaying number of F-14s have

been lost in engine-related incidents. The Navy will soon take delivery of its first F-14Ds, with a state-of-the-art digital cockpit and vastly more satisfactory General Electric F-110 fan engines. "Let me get my hands on the D-model," enthuses former Top Gun instructor Comdr. C. J. "Heater" Heatley, "and there won't be a fighter on the planet that can stick with me."

With the Phantom relegated to fading photographs on the walls of the Top Gun classrooms, the only other player, taking up the remaining third of each class, is the new McDonnell-Douglas/Northrop F-18 Hornet. The F-18 has only been in attendance at Top Gun for a short time, but it has already established itself as the bird to beat.

The F-18 grew out of the Air Force's lightweight fighter competition of the early seventies. The F-16 won the marbles, including sales numbering in the hundreds to a number of NATO allies. The YF-17 was the loser. But the Navy liked its two-engine configuration (the F-16 is a one-holer) and it soon transmogrified into the F/A-18.

A Tomcat of Miramar Squadron VF-211 test-fires a million-dollar AIM-54A Phoenix missile off the southern California coast.

The Pentagon's history with multi-role aircraft has been less than impressive. Most have turned out to be overweight, overly complex, over budget, and not particularly good at any of their multiple missions. The dual-role Hornet has proven to be the sparkling and long-awaited exception.

The operational F-18 looks a lot like the YF-17 prototype, but light and simple it's not. In the first place, it's "navalized" – beefed up and corrosion-proofed for carrier ops. Then has come system after system – top-notch Hughes APG-65 digital multi-mode radar, FLIR (forward-looking infrared) for night vision, fly-by-wire computer-aided flight controls, digital panel with most displays on a trio of CRT screens, ever-evolving software to make everything come together. The result is heavy, complicated, and God-awfully expensive. But it *works*.

As either a fighter or an attack bomber, the F/A-18 apologizes to no aircraft on earth. It turns with scooters like the F-16; it pitches vertical like nothing this side of Cape Canaveral. Pilots praise its superb visibility, its computer-assisted handling, and its brilliantly engineered cockpit. In the attack role, it gives the carrier strike package a supersonic bomber that can deliver either "smart" or "iron dumb" ordnance with computer-controlled accuracy beyond the imagination of Phantom-era mud movers. And at the flick of a button on the radar, the attack puke switches back to dogfight mode for the possible fight coming off the target.

Hidden in the Hornet's high cost are two enormous benefits. First, it's unbelievably easy to learn to fly. True proficiency in the Phantom took years of sweat; the Hornet makes novices feel comfortable in minutes. The Phantom could be driven, in balls-to-the-wall ACM, over the edge into flat-spin departures from which there was no salvation other than the Nylon Letdown. No one has yet succeeded in putting the Hornet into an

A VF-124 Tomcat shows off its amazing ability to bat-turn at high-G and low speed.

attitude from which it can't recover. Indeed, its computer controls can be relied on to figure out the right moves even if the disoriented pilot can't. The drill in case of "bad SA" (loss of situational awareness) is literally to let go of the stick and permit the plane to recover itself.

In my usual dilettante fashion I've flown F-4s (Air Force models have dual controls) and F-18s for perhaps a total of an hour each. In the Phantom I never got beyond trying to hold heading and altitude. In the Hornet, I was getting away with honest-to-God aerobatics after 20 minutes. In many respects the F-18 is easier to fly than your dentist's Beech Bonanza.

The Hornet's other great hidden benefit is its reliability and freedom from maintenance. Man hours per flight hour are a tiny fraction of the norm for the Phantoms and A-7 Corsairs it replaces. (I know, I know; lighten up on the poor Phantom already!) I recently joined a detachment of eight Marine Hornets while they put in two weeks of ACM fun and games with Air Force Reserve F-16s. The eight jets were up and 100 percent trouble free for the entire period, three and four hops a day. The Jarheads just climbed in and turned the key, to the amazement of the Falcon drivers. They thought they had it good, just having transitioned from the beloved but trouble-prone F-105 "Thud," yet their F-16s clearly needed far more stroking and tweaking than the (admittedly brand-new) Hornets.

Against the students' enormously capable and reliable fourth-generation fighters the Top Gun staff fields a squadron of agile, no-frills aircraft from another era. The school's prime mover is the Northrop F-5E Tiger II, a small, lightweight

fighter originally designed for export to allies that didn't need, or couldn't afford to operate, the latest and hottest fighters. The American military never made any use of the F-5 except as an adversary trainer for dissimilar air combat. The famed Air Force Aggressor squadrons also use the F-5, specifically to simulate the Soviet MiG-21, which it closely resembles in size (small) and flying characteristics (nothing to write Mom about). The quintet of dreaded Commie "MiG-28s" in the movie *Top Gun* were F-5s borrowed from Top Gun, done up in wash-off black latex paint, and flown by four Top Gun jocks plus Rear Admiral Tom "Baron" Cassidy.

The F-5 is a beautiful, sexy airplane, with a needle nose, razor-thin straight wings, and two small GE J-85 afterburning engines of 5,000 pounds thrust each. Controls are manual and unassisted, although powered maneuvering flaps can be dropped from leading and trailing edges to improve cornering rates. The control panel is simpler than that of many private planes—no radar (Air Force Aggressors do carry a crude radar), minimal IFR instrumentation, no weapons systems other than a simple gunsight. Its afterburners give the F-5 supersonic capability, but only in bursts of a few seconds; the little jet carries very little gas, and its "short legs" are a continuing problem in Top Gun's more complex multi-plane hops. On one of our photo rides in a two-seat F-5F, we came up against air-traffic de-

Transonic vapor hovering above the wing roots, an F/A-18 Hornet reefs effortlessly into the pure vertical in a Top Gun dogfight.

The dirt-simple panel of the F-5 Tiger. Southern California radio frequencies are listed at right. Many private single-engine planes sport more exotic instrument displays.

lays on our return to Miramar. Even though we had been careful with power settings and had stayed completely out of burner during the one-hour ride, we still had to make an emergency low-fuel landing at NAS El Centro, disrupting and pissing off the practicing Blue Angels in the process. Although the F-5 can be configured for in-flight refueling, the Top Gun Tigers are not.

The F-5's Top Gun stablemate is the A-4E Skyhawk, a thirty-year-old attack design that is still being used by, among others, the Israelis, the Argentines, and the U.S. Marines as a tough light bomber. The Top Gun Skyhawks are "Mongoose" variants, stripped of all nonessential weight and equipped with the big Pratt P-8 engine putting out almost 11,000 pounds of thrust. The Blue Angels are flying similar souped-up versions, at least until they take delivery of the spectacular F-18 in early 1987.

Marine F/A-18 makes life miserable for an Air Force F-16 over the Yuma TACTS Range.

The Mongoose supposedly simulates the ancient Soviet MiG-17, although its dogfighting performance is far superior. The A-4E is actually a potent ACM scrapper, able, in the right hands, to give any aircraft the chills in a close-in fight. It turns like crazy, it has a surprising reserve of energy for vertical maneuvers, it stays in the fight at slower speeds, and it has a responsive, untemperamental flying personality. Plus it shares one of a fighter's most desired virtues with the F-5; both are tiny and hard to see, especially for a Fleet F-14 Tomcat driver who's been flying mostly against his hulking squadron mates. Check the cover shot of the two Top Gun jets forming on the F-14 — the wingspan of each is smaller than the Turkey's tail. The Mongoose is determinedly subsonic, lacking an afterburner and high-speed air intakes. But it's really no problem since few dogfights take place beyond the sound barrier.

Israeli Kfir, designated F-21 by the Navy, is being operated as an interim adversary fighter on the East Coast and out of MCAS Yuma.

The Top Gun staffers, and the professional Gomers in the Navy's adversary squadrons, fly the A-4 and F-5 MiG simulators (plus the two-seat T-38 Talon, a very close cousin of the F-5) far beyond their modest paper profiles. It is virtually unheard of for a new Top Gun student to defeat an instructor in the first few 1 V 1 engagements, despite the superiority of his mount. Of course, these are simple visual setups, with rules of engagement that negate the long-range intercept capabilities of the student aircraft. And when the students start picking up on the lessons — the learning curve shoots up dramatically as the course progresses — the instructors have a steadily harder time staying alive. That, of course, is the idea.

The Top Gun pilots can make their A-4s and F-5s perform amazing feats, but the little birds will only go so far. More sophisticated and capable adversary aircraft are needed; although there are countless thousands of MiG-17s, -19s, and -21s flying all over the world, far more serious threats are replacing them. The Soviet "RAM" series of fighters, expected to mirror more closely the capabilities of the American teen fighters, are now entering active service within the Warsaw Pact. Modern French fighters such as the fly-by-wire Mirage 2000 are being sold to God knows whom. Top Gun and the adversary outfits have to upgrade.

On an interim basis, the east coast Gomers are now flying leased Israeli Kfirs. The Kfir (we're calling it the F-21) is something of a Jewish Mirage, having been concocted from stolen French plans. It's supersonic, a pretty good angles fighter with excellent energy. And it even *looks* Russian, with its long nose probe and chunky Flogger-like tail.

The permanent upgrade for both Top Gun and the adversary/composite squadrons will be a special version of the General Dynamics F-16 with lots of power but minimal weapons systems. Top Gun will get the first of its half-dozen F-16Ns in spring 1987. The little Falcon is by all measurements a superb good-weather dogfighter, undoubtedly the equal of anything in the sky. The Top Gun gang can hardly wait.

Excited as they are about strapping on the F-16 "Electric Jet," many of the instructors will admit, more or less off the record, that it wouldn't be their first pick for a new fighter. Although politics, economics, and other boring aspects of reality place it currently out of the running, the new Northrop F-20 Tigershark would have been the boys' number-one choice. Top Gun would love to continue with a follow-on Northrop fighter, having had such excellent service from the F-5, and even the F-20's detractors admit that it's every bit as hot in a dogfight as the F-16 while being far cheaper to acquire and operate. But the privately developed Tigershark has yet to make a strong enough sale to start up the production line, and nothing very encouraging is on the horizon. It's a sad, sad, hard-luck story; don't get me started on it. Suffice it to say that short of a miracle the F-20 won't be signing on at Top Gun. But the F-16 is a hell of a substitute, able to stick with and stick it to any student, regardless of how well he has learned his lessons.

But enough of hardware. Let's get airborne and find out how this game is played. After all, how hard can it be? Harder, it turns out, than most of us can possibly imagine. Time to go to school.

Artist Ed Moore's conception of the soon-to-be-delivered Top Gun F-16N. Bird sports dummy Sidewinder missile on left station, and data pod for transmitting information to TACTS system on right station.

Fight's On

The Blue Angels and the *Top Gun* movie stars make it all look effortless, but the difficulties of hammering a jet fighter around in three dimensions can only be hinted at in words. There is no substitute for an actual hop in the back seat, something few civilians ever get to experience. We're going to "qualify" and go along for a ride.

The Navy requires recurrent survival training for everyone who flies in its aircraft, active-duty, reserve, or civilian. There are a smattering of exceptions; journalists and VIP guests are flown to and from carriers on helicopters or COD (Carrier On-Board Delivery) aircraft, and a handful of the famous and fortunate are taken up for short hops in the Blue Angels' lone two-seat Skyhawk. Everyone else is expected to punch the necessary tickets in a physiology training (FASO) outfit.

Current FASO training takes up the best part of two days. Lectures the first day cover the perils of hypoxia (oxygen starvation or narcosis), spatial disorientation, and the various effects of diet on vision and cockpit comfort. Jet pilots and crew segue in the afternoon into an altitude or decompression chamber, to review the workings of the universal oxygen systems and to experience the onset of hypoxia. Masks are removed at an "altitude" of 35,000 feet, and the subjects play simple games (puzzles, patty cake) until they begin to make giggling fools of themselves.

A terrible problem with hypoxia is that it is difficult to recognize in oneself. Some people feel giddy and carefree; others suffer horrifying hallucinations. Oxygen-starved jet pilots have been known to fly into the ground, laughing all the way down, oblivious to the frantic calls of wingmen. It's a terrifying possibility, especially in the single-seat jets.

The altitude chamber session is usually concluded with a bang — a rapid decompression blasts everyone instantly back to sea level, scaring the bejesus out of the uninitiated. Undoubtedly the real thing in a high-flying aircraft, tactical jet or big transport, would be a lot more frightening still.

Day two at FASO gets rough. Plan on a full, tiring day in the water. Everyone kicks off with swimming tests in a large, deep outdoor pool. After warming up with a demonstrated ability in several different strokes, pilots and crew are suited up in their flying garb — flight suits, boots, helmets and survival vests for the prop and helo people, an added G-suit layer for the attack and fighter boys. All hands are expected to swim seventy-five yards, three laps of the pool, in gear that gets more cumbersome and water-logged with each stroke. Next come fifteen nonstop minutes of "drown-proofing," the modern Navy version of treading water. *Now* everyone is permitted to pull the twin toggles and fire his inflatable LPA, or life vest.

Next a battery of diabolical gadgets come into play. There's the "Dilbert Dunker," a mock jet cockpit on an angled track. It rolls inverted about ten feet beneath the water, at which time the occupant must unhook and swim to the surface. Do the Dilbert twice, once blindfolded — chances are the visibility in the water will be absolute zero in a real disaster.

Everyone adjourns to an immense indoor pool

Previous spread: Student-flown F-14 gets seriously mad at an instructor's F-5 over China Lake.

54

to experience the "Helo Dunker"—panic in a drum. A large cylindrical simulation of a CH-46 "Frog" helicopter fuselage slides down a forty-five-degree track into the pool; cams rotate the drum, bringing it to a stop *inverted* about twelve feet under. Wait for violent motion to cease (the drum hits the water hard), unhook and swim out your window. Fun? You bet! How about giving it three more tries? Ride number two: Everyone swims out a single front entry door, and a form of musical chairs ensues as grown men and women fight for the seat nearest the door. Okay, gang,

twice more, once out your own window, once out the main door, *blindfolded*, no peeking. The Helo Dunker is an excellent and enormously worthwhile drill, brought into being after a rash of tragic CH-46 ditchings. The twin-rotor helo, widely used by both Navy and Marines for blue-water ops, carries much of its weight up high in its

Navy aircrews are required to undergo recurrent training in such devices as the "Dilbert Dunker," a mock jet cockpit from which the pilot must escape underwater.

engines and transmission. In the water it turns turtle instantly and sinks like a cinder block. Even with the Helo Dunker experience the FASO instructors admit that escape from a ditched Frog is problematical.

FASO day two wraps up with other amusing diversions—a parachute drag before a huge wind machine (unhook those tricky Koch fittings before the wet chute pulls you under), a helo rescue lift (work yourself into the dangling harness as another wind machine blows spray in your face), pull yourself into a seven-man raft. Harsh as FASO training is, you get the distinct (and reportedly accurate) impression that none of the simula-

tions are even a fraction as rough as the real thing would be. Imagine a cloudy night, mountainous seas, bitter water temperatures, the strong possibility of injuries during the ejection or crash. FASO training or no, no one jokes about, or looks forward to, a forced departure from the airplane.

Ejection from a high-performance aircraft is preferable to sticking around, but it's never a picnic. There are no practice ejections—if you do it,

---

Navy/Marine CH-46 Frog, although generally reliable in two decades of service, doesn't do very well in water ditchings. "Helo Dunker" training helps aircrews prepare for quick escape from a Frog in the water.

you do it for real. Even the most user-friendly rocket seats, such as the F-18's superb ACES II, let fly with a 12-G jolt; next comes a face-to-face with hundreds of knots of slipstream. Some injury is almost inevitable—compressed vertebrae, broken wrists from flailing arms, black eyes.

Much depends on the airplane's speed. If the problem is a deteriorating one, such as a gradual loss of control due to hydraulic failure, the crew might well have time to get organized for the blow-out, giving Mayday and location on the radio, last-second tightening of straps and belts, securing loose articles, pitch up to bleed airspeed, perhaps even dropping the flaps, hook and wheels to bring the speed down under one hundred knots. Piece of cake. The other extreme is vastly more perilous, with no guarantee of survival. A catastrophic emergency at realistic tactical speeds—midair collision, engine explosion, enemy missile hit—leaves the pilot with nanoseconds to pull the Loud Handle and take his chances. Serious injury will almost certainly result, but there's not much of a choice. The majority of American jet pilots taken prisoner in Vietnam were hurt somehow during their ejections, greatly compounding their suffering in captivity.

There's seldom much time to mull over an ejection. A TA-4 Skyhawk recently lost all power over San Diego Bay on final to NAS North Island. As the jet rolled inverted, one of the crew pulled the plug. The seats were preset to fire in sequence,

Two Naval Reserve Tomcats go at it off the California coast. Survival and ejection techniques must become instinctive— there is little time in an emergency to decide what to do, and no chance to do it over.

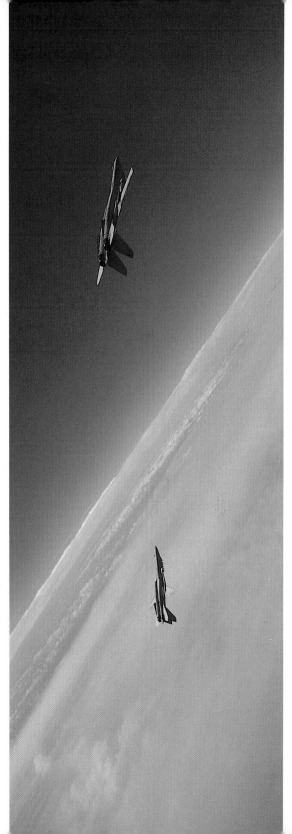

Tomcat takes a break between ACM tussles to top off from a convenient Naval Reserve KA-3 Whale aerial tanker.

rear seat first, 0.4 seconds apart. The woman NFO in the back seat got one good swing of her chute and hit the water okay. The pilot, blowing out less than a half second later, was fired ballistically into the water. He died instantly.

We'll hope for better things. We're "qualed" for an orientation hop in the back seat of an F-14, with the folks at Miramar's Reserve Squadron VF-302, the Stallions, doing the honors. A serious young petty officer, one of the unit's survival equipment specialists, gives us the gouge on the Tomcat's Martin-Baker ejection seat and the dozens of ingenious gadgets that are packed into the survival

vest and raft. It never hurts, he advises, to sit calmly at the end of the runway, just before beginning the takeoff roll, and mime the procedure once more: loose articles stowed, straps supertight, good body position, head back, both hands on the overhead handles, boom. This Could Be The Day.

We'll be doing some air-to-air photography on this flight, and we'll also be meeting up with a

RAG Tomcat for a couple of visual 1 V 1 dog-fights. We're flying with squadron skipper John Ed "Tiger" Kerr, a Vietnam combat vet and former Top Gun instructor who now flies Western Airlines 727s when he's not blasting around in his Tomcat. Tiger is a compact, balding man with a perennial smile on his face. He supervises me strapping into the back seat, and he shows me a few radio and nav responsibilities I'll have to cover on the preflight checklist. The Tomcat is a true two-man airplane, even though the back-seater, in the Navy tradition, has no flight controls.

We join our wingman at the end of the active runway and run through the final checks. A bandit TA-4 and a Hawkeye wait in line in front of us. We pull the safety pins from our ejection seats, arming the rockets. On my mind is a bizarre accident that had happened on the deck of the USS *Enterprise* a few days before. A Tomcat had just trapped and taxied forward after a routine mission. As the pilot and RIO unhooked and climbed from the cockpit, the seats mysteriously fired in murderous sequence. Both men died. F-14 pilots at Miramar were baffled by this horrible accident.

Clearance at last. Our two Tomcats take the active for a section go. Tiger pushes the throttles forward to military power and beyond into maximum afterburner: Zone V. He pops the brakes, and the huge jet lurches forward. Acceleration is smooth but devastating; we're off the deck and rolling into a right turn as we pass the three-thousand-foot mark. The end-of-runway gun-testing tunnel flashes by on our right. It is festooned with the slogan "WELCOME TO FIGHTERTOWN USA." We climb easily through the last of the morning fog and clouds; the low stuff usually burns off at Miramar before noon. In no time we're over the Pacific and

through 10,000 feet; the variable-sweep wings roll back to fifty degrees. Out here we're talking CAVU — clear air, visibility unlimited.

Our dash-two, with Jeff "Fang" Punches up front and flight surgeon/RIO Connie "Doc" Ward in the back, slides up neatly on our sunny side for some snapshots. After some steep turns, an effortless formation loop, and some masks-off mugging for the camera, our pals clear out for another mission. We find a loitering E-2 Hawkeye and talk its crew into posing for some shots. Then it's time to take on some gas from a handy Reserve KA-3 "Whale" tanker before changing frequencies and hooking up with our adversary.

We'll be flying against VF-124's Lt. Comdr. (now commander and squadron executive officer) Chuck "Heater" Heatley, former Top Gun teacher, terrific photographer, and acknowledged 1 V 1 master. Tiger is a veteran of air combat in Vietnam; Heater joined the Navy a bit late to see action, but in his four years on the Top Gun faculty he set himself to learning as much about the zen of 1 V 1 as any pilot anywhere. His efforts have paid off: fighter pilots throughout the Navy, an egotistical lot, single him out as the man to beat. His 1 V 1 "master class" in the West Coast RAG has even passed a few new tricks on to the current Top Gun syllabus.

Tiger and Heater haven't briefed their moves; we'll see who surprises whom. We're going to set up line abreast and a mile apart for two quick visual fights. Tiger suggests I peer into the radar. Heater is dead ahead at ten miles. Tiger has him visual; despite an RIO's patient ground briefing, I'm getting nothing but clutter and a few distant targets on my radar screen.

Seconds later we flash past each other, a few hundred feet apart, closure speed up around

"Lose sight, lose the fight": Your intrepid scribe, at the controls of a Top Gun F-5F, intently scans the wrong half of the sky as a student F-14 tracks for a painfully easy guns kill.

1,100 knots. Tiger pulls us vertical; as we load up past 3 Gs, my G-suit constricts urgently around my legs and queasy gut. I try to look over my shoulder for Heater. Even at a relatively mild 3 Gs, the effort causes sweat to pour into my eyes. He's nowhere in sight—at least not with my lousy vision. We go to zero, then negative G as we roll inverted across the top. A half-roll and everything's right-side-up again as we scream down toward our set-up altitude. Tiger allows the jet to slip past Mach 1; we're no doubt rattling some portholes down on the water, but there isn't the slightest clue in the cockpit.

We slide into a loose line-abreast formation with Heater at 22,000 feet—same direction, same altitude, a bit more than a mile apart. His big jet is plainly visible at this distance. We're duplicating a Top Gun student's first few hops—formal 1 V 1 visual setups with both aircraft starting on an equal footing. The student gets to fly his plane to the edge of the envelope; the instructor gets an idea of the sort of moves the student has up his sleeve. This is the essence of 1 V 1: probing the limits of your opponent, your jet, and yourself.

I get to drop the puck on the ice. Tiger warns me to put my head back into the headrest, then to key the mike and transmit the universal code phrase. I hear myself distantly in the headphones calling, "Fight's on."

I'm squashed into the seat by a "fangs out" 6-G bat-turn to the left, and we hurtle straight at each other. This is the approved opening gambit, Boelke's Rule Number Six, the equivalent of the all-or-nothing snap at the start of a wrist wrestling match. At the pass a scant few seconds later, the real fun begins. We snap-roll 180 degrees to cross canopy-to-canopy. I catch a glimpse of Heater's afterburners and full wing sweep. He has the

hammer down, "going for knots." I lose sight immediately; my head goes down and stays down as we pull another 6-G turn to try for his six. "Got him in sight?" asks Tiger calmly. You've got to be kidding. A lot of good I'd be at this job.

The Gs lessen as we slide out of the turn. Another 180-degree snap-roll, and there's Heater, turning about 75 degrees away from us, burners still cooking. Tiger not only flies and fights, he also provides the breezy play-by-play, without which I wouldn't have any idea what's up. "He's holding maximum sustained turn rate, 340 knots," says Tiger. Talk about reading your adversary's energy state. "Hang on—turning inside for a shot." Six Gs again. I sink into the seat, sweat pouring from under my too-big helmet. This is not fun.

Tiger mutters to himself: "Come on, John, get it." We're manhandling the big jet into Fox Two parameters—Sidewinder shot into those glowing burners. Heater keeps motoring at best rate, but our tight radius is costing us our energy. We have to get off a shot before we're out of Schlitz.

Heater is foxing us, of course. A second before our shot, he rolls wings level, drops the nose for a moment, then reefs the 'Cat into a mind-boggling pure vertical climb. He pulls away like a Saturn V. Tiger mumbles the fighter pilot's prayer: "Oh, shit." We can't get the nose up on him, even for an instant—no energy. We hammerhead over, and the blue Pacific fills the canopy. "Try to eyeball him," says Tiger resignedly. "He'll be dropping in on us." I look back between the twin tails as we unload. No joy: I'm sure he's there, but my eyesight isn't up to the job.

We hear Heater's calm "Fox Two on the Tomcat" as we pull out to honor the 10,000-foot hard deck. We're a "mort." I'm thinking about the

French toast I had for breakfast; I fear I'm going to be seeing it again any moment. A glance at my $10 Casio digital tells me that the fight has lasted a shade under one minute.

OK, so the guy is good. We set up for another go. I grit my teeth and call "Fight's on" again. Another God-awful bat-turn, and this time it's our turn to go full macho Zone V burner. Once again we snap-roll 180 degrees into Heater to keep from losing sight. Trouble again. Tiger says, "Godammit, idle and boards." Translation: our wily adversary has cut his throttles and popped his "boards," or speed brakes. He's digging into a 6-G nose-low-and-dead-slow turn, hanging in the sky like the Goodyear blimp. Before we know it, Heater's at our 8-o'clock 3,000 feet away. Definitely not good. ("I do that number, I'm like a machine gun

in a shopping cart—for a few seconds I can point anywhere," crows Heater in the post-flight debrief. We find out that he even dropped his landing flaps!)

We have to defeat his gun solution. Tiger stomps in a bootful of left rudder; violent yaw hurls me against the right canopy as we plummet into something called a "high-G roll underneath." I'm beginning to hate this. Heater blessedly calls "knock it off" as we come up once again on the hard deck. "Great guns defense!" Heater calls on the radio. Thanks a lot.

Vapor signals severe positive G as a Tomcat lights the pipes and pulls for the vertical.

We're coming up, thank sweet Jesus, on bingo fuel; time to head for the barn. We join in a tight welded wing for the quick ride back to Miramar. The cockpit is cool, but I'm drenched in sweat and the backs of my flying gloves are saturated from wiping my forehead. I avoided throwing up, but not by much. My jaw aches from clenching my teeth. Less than ten minutes of let's-pretend ACM, and I feel as though I've gone the distance with Marvelous Marv. I drag out the Nikon and take some shots of Heater to get my mind off my misery. Wise guy—he has *his* Nikon out, and he's shooting us. We tighten the formation for a bad-to-the-bone break over the Miramar runway; the fighter pilot's credo is to look good at all times, at all costs. Heater snap-turns at midfield. We count five seconds and follow him around. One last 4-G burst, and then we're downwind with the wings racked out to full forward. The huge jet floats in on final, seemingly no faster over the fence than a single-engine Cessna.

I've ridden along on perhaps ten ACM hops—some with easy set-ups for my edification, some with no holds barred—and in every case I have spent most of the ride in a nauseous daze. I don't know whether to laugh or cry at my pilot's polite inquiries, "Got a tally on our bad guy? Got his wingman? Got *our* wingman? Isn't this neat?"

When people ask me, "Boy, wasn't that fun?" my usual answer is that the experience is many things—exciting, dynamic, enervating, the ride of a lifetime, an E ticket. But *fun*? Fighter pilots think it's fun, but they do it every day, they're used to it, they *understand* it. It's not particularly frightening; it's clear the pilots know their stuff, and safety is paramount even in the most furious engagements. I'm usually too confused and miserable to be scared. On one particularly ghastly 9-G F-16 fight I would have cheerfully welcomed death. That pilots and back-seaters can function in this environment, can retain perfect situational awareness and prevail in the fight, still astonishes me. Paramount's *Top Gun* tried mightily to put some of this across to the casual observer, but the surface was barely scratched.

Soaking up Gs is an acquired skill. Some knuckleheads like Heater Heatley actually claim to enjoy the sensation. Pilots often build up a tolerance for 7 and 8 Gs; if they're away from the dogfighting business for a few weeks, they have to ease back into things with a few flights of nothing more than 5 Gs sustained. Many pilots and RIOs are surprisingly (or not so surprisingly) beefy, with football player necks and thickly muscled torsos. A daily diet of ACM is probably better

than pumping iron for tightening up the bod. I once got caught with my head down, changing film, when my F-15 pilot loaded us up into a sudden 6.5-G turn. I literally couldn't lift my noggin, which probably weighed in at 150 pounds with the helmet. That was about four months ago, just one so-so snap turn in one fight, and my neck still bothers me today.

Back on the deck, Heater launches into a dissertation on one of his favorite topics: 1 V 1, the distillation of air combat, the skill that is utterly central to ACM regardless of the number of planes involved. "In a sense, it's *all* 1 V 1 up there.

Down on the deck at China Lake, a student F-14 chases a Top Gun F-5 at 400 knots. Probably a sucker play, with another instructor sneaking up at six o'clock!

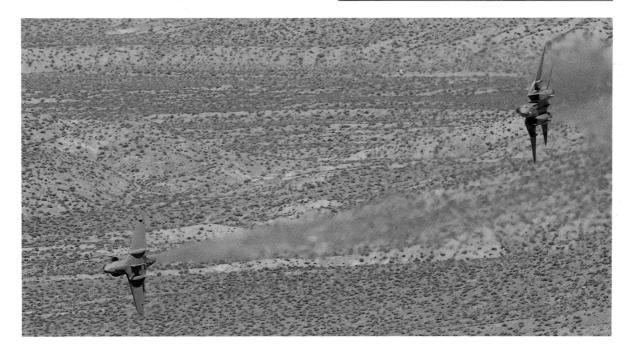

If you're converging on a guy in a big furball, you're 1 V 1 with him. If some Commie taxies in on your eight o'clock and squeezes off a missile, you're suddenly 1 V 1 with that missile. Evade that threat, and you're going to find yourself 1 V 1 with your bad guy again, as he tries to close for a gun attack. If you really, really learn to fight 1 V 1, you'll develop the skill and confidence in the airplane to survive and prevail in the multi-bogey engagements."

The Top Gun students' first five hops are 1 V 1s, visual fights starting off co-heading and co-altitude; after the first week the fights will be set up on radar intercept and ground control, a far more realistic scenario. Although the students' F-14s and F-18s are the superior machines, they are nevertheless likely to get thrashed in these early engagements. It all depends on how much the student already knows about ACM, and how much actual practice he's had in recent weeks. Fleet pilots and Marine F-18 drivers fly a myriad of different missions — fleet defense, day and night carrier qualification, radar intercepts, aerial refueling, instrument work, low-level attack and bombing practice in the Hornet communities. ACM is just one of many mission profiles. If the student's outfit has just cycled through FARP (Fleet ACM Readiness Program) training, he's liable to be a pretty current dogfighter. Also some squadrons send their fair-haired crews off to Top Gun with a bunch of practice hops in which the outfit's best dogfighters pass along their favorite tips and tricks.

Still, the instructors tend to be a quantum leap ahead of the best students the first few times out. A former Top Gun skipper likened their relative capabilities to those of an Olympic medal winner versus a top high school athlete. "I flew nothing but ACM for four years at Top Gun, a couple of hops a day, three or four engagements on each hop," remembers Heatley. "We had all our moves down to the Nth degree. We could read a student's energy state to a whisker. We knew what he was thinking before he thought it.

"The F-14 guy on the boat, he has to fit ACM in with a lot of other missions, and when he does fight it's likely to be with another Tomcat. He's making mistakes of a hundred knots in airspeed, he's missing angles, he's wasting energy, one day he wins, next day he loses. He comes to Top Gun and the guy's on a different planet. Be twenty-five knots off on your airspeed, be inefficient on your reversals, lose sight of that little teeny F-5 for a split second, and you're going to be dead."

The science of air combat maneuvering — and it is a science as well as an art — is difficult to explain in words and two-dimensional diagrams. Navy fighter pilot Robert Shaw has done a remarkably thorough job, however, in his book *Fighter Combat;* I strongly recommend it to serious students of aerial tactics and maneuver. It occasionally reads like a dense physics text, but then there's a lot of physics wrapped up in what an airplane can and cannot do in a fight. The most basic engagement maneuver, what the pilots call "lift vector and pull" (the lift vector is an imaginary vertical plane extending out from the top of your canopy; bank to place the lift vector on your adversary, and pull into him with the control stick), is one of literally thousands of possible fighter maneuvers. For specific descriptions of the different maneuvers — rolling scissors, high and low yo-yo's, lead turns, defensive splits and the like — I refer the dedicated reader to Shaw's lucid descriptions and fascinating asides.

Mixed in among the equations and ribbon diagrams are hundreds of wonderfully applicable quotations from history's greatest fighter pilots, like this recollection from World War II ace Robert Johnson, probably the greatest P-47 Jug pilot ever. The encounter described is a mock engagement over England between Johnson's heavy Thunderbolt and a new Mark-IX Spitfire, an airplane with both power-to-weight and wing-loading advantages over the ponderous Jug:

We flew together in formation, and then I decided to see what this new airplane had to its credit.

I opened the throttle full and the Thunderbolt forged ahead. A moment later exhaust smoke poured from the Spit as the pilot came after me. He couldn't make it; the big Jug had a definite speed advantage. I grinned happily; I'd heard so much about this airplane that I really wanted to show off the Thunderbolt to her pilot. The Jug kept

Instructor Sandy "Jaws" Winnefeld rehashes an engagement with F-15 driver Mike "Boa" Straight, Top Gun's first Air Force instructor. Scale models are commonly used to re-create maneuvers in the debrief.

pulling away from the Spitfire; suddenly I hauled back on the stick and lifted the nose. The Thunderbolt zoomed upward, soaring into the cloud-flecked sky. I looked out and back; the Spit was straining to match me, and barely able to hold his position.

But my advantage was only the zoom—once in steady climb, he had me. I gaped as smoke poured from the exhausts and the Spitfire shot past me as if I were standing still. Could that plane climb! He tore upward in a climb I couldn't match in the Jug. Now it was his turn; the broad elliptical wings rolled, swung around, and the Spit screamed in, hell-bent on chewing me up.

This was going to be fun. I knew he could turn inside the heavy Thunderbolt; if I attempted to hold a tight turn the Spitfire would slip right inside me. I knew, also, that he could easily outclimb my fighter. I stayed out of those sucker traps. First

Above: Hornet puffs vapor as it pulls maximum G in the horizontal. *Right:* Dogfighting maestro "Heater" Heatley yanks his Turkey over the top as more transonic vapor erupts above the wings.

rule in this kind of fight: don't fight the way your opponent fights best. No sharp turns; don't climb; keep him at your level.

We were at 5,000 feet, the Spitfire skidding around hard and coming in on my tail. No use turning: he'd whip right inside me as if I were a truck loaded with cement, and snap out in firing position. Well, I had a few tricks too. The P-47 was faster, and I threw the ship into a roll. Right here I had him. The Jug could outroll any plane in the air, bar none. With my speed, roll was my only advantage, and I made full use of the manner in which the Thunderbolt could whirl. I kicked the Jug into a wicked left roll, horizon spinning

crazily, once, twice, into a third. As he turned to the left to follow, I tramped down on the right rudder, banged the stick over to the right. Around and around we went, left, right, left, right. I could whip through two rolls before the Spitfire even completed his first. And this killed his ability to turn inside me. I just refused to turn. Every time he tried to follow me in a roll, I flashed away to the opposite side, opening the gap between our two planes.

Then I played the trump. The Spitfire was clawing wildly through the air, trying to follow me in a roll, when I dropped the nose. The Thunderbolt howled and ran for earth. Barely had the Spitfire started to follow — and I was a long way ahead of him now — when I jerked back on the stick and threw the Jug into a zoom climb. In a straight or turning climb, the British ship had the advantage. But coming out of a dive, there's not a British or German fighter that can come close to a Thunderbolt rushing upward in a zoom. Before the Spit pilot knew what had happened, I was high above him, the Thunderbolt hammering around. And that was it — for in the next few moments the Spitfire flier was amazed to see a less maneuverable, slower-climbing Thunderbolt rushing straight at him, eight guns pointed ominously at his cockpit.

Virtually all the key lessons of air combat can be gleaned from this all-out fight between two professionals. Above all, Johnson has controlled the fight by using his plane's limited advantages and denying his opponent the full employment of his mount's far superior dogfighting capabilities. Johnson maintains a chin-out offense ("don't fight the way your opponent fights best"), switching to defensive rolls to baffle his bogey and keep him from gaining angles. Then comes the dive, zoom climb and hammerhead (what Shaw calls a "div-

69

ing extension and pitch-back") to regain the offensive and use energy tactics to thrash a "double superior" (better power-to-weight plus lighter wing-loading) opponent. The Top Gun guys couldn't have pulled it off any better.

Fighter pilots constantly throw about the terms "angles" and "energy." Out come the knife-edge hands, one above and behind the other, the boys shooting down their wristwatches. The terms are hard to explain, but they're at the heart of ACM and the understanding thereof.

Gaining angles involves using the aircraft's turning abilities to the maximum, "pulling on the pole" to place one's fighter in the best possible shooting position—on the bogey's dead six. The relative angles difference, then, is expressed in the number of degrees each plane must turn to get zero angles on the other. Gaining an energy advantage involves the manipulation of the fighter's speed and momentum to build and store energy that can be converted into a shooting position. Most fights will involve a fluid combination of both techniques.

The rub is that angles and energy are somewhat incompatible. Tight turning reduces speed and dissipates energy, whereas speeding or zooming to gain energy greatly widens turn rates. Pretty basic physics here—these rules hold constant for any and all aircraft. The fighter pilot must make a running stream of angles versus energy decisions, and a definite instinct is required. The pilot might opt for a speed some forty knots above best cornering rate, knowing that his bird will only give up one degree per second in turn rate. Not a bad trade-off at first glance. But how long is the average ACM engagement? One to two minutes, say the experts; let's split the difference at ninety seconds. But wait a minute, our pilot is giving up

ninety degrees of angles for a bit more speed. A canny angles opponent will take those ninety degrees and stick them where the sun doesn't shine. But a descending run to build speed, energy and separation may not be the answer either—not in the era of the Mach-4 air-to-air missile. The modern dogfighter must make constant microsecond reevaluations in that one or two minutes of air combat.

Dogfighting is often referred to as a three-dimensional chess game, with a countermove for every move. It's actually more of a three-dimensional billiards game. In chess, the number of possible moves is undoubtedly in the billions, but it is a finite number. In billiards, as in ACM, the number of movement options is an analog infinity.

The best fighters allow tight turning while maintaining good speed and energy; it's currently hard to beat the F-18 in this regard. The big F-14, if allowed to drop under 250 knots in a high-altitude turning or angles fight, will wallow near uncontrollability, its engines doing little more than converting kerosene into noise. One age-old trick is to descend while turning at maximum corner rate, thus using gravity to inject some energy into the turn. Of course, the pilot who tries this trick for too long will find himself going 1 V 1 with the ground—never a winning proposition.

A collision with the ground, or another airplane, isn't the only kind of catastrophe a fighter pilot has to anticipate in a mock dogfight. The ever-present danger in flying at the edge of the envelope is slipping *outside* the envelope. Any aircraft—Piper Cub, Concorde, or F-14—has maximum performance parameters beyond which its pilot should venture only at his great peril. A fighter's maximum positive G rating, for instance,

can be exceeded by an overexcited pilot in a tight turn, but it's not a great idea; structural damage can result, and the airplane can literally fold up if it is stressed beyond certain limits. This danger is exceedingly remote in modern jets, but a number of World War I fighters suffered fatal wing failures in combat. More likely in the eighties is the dreaded "departure," in which the airplane steps outside the realm of controlled flight.

Any airfoil will stall and stop lifting the airplane if the angle of attack (the angle of the wing

Painted up in imaginary squadron markings for the film *Top Gun*, "Iceman's" F-14 is joined by "Viper's" Mongoose during air-to-air filming at NAS Fallon, Nevada.

cross-section relative to direction of flight) becomes too great; air can no longer move over the top of the airfoil to generate lift. In the best of circumstances, a stalling airplane with wings level will simply nose over and eat up a bit of altitude before recovering into normal flight. A dogfight, however, comes close to the worst of circumstances. If a high-performance jet should

Author's rear-looking remote camera pod catches dramatic view of VF-302 Tomcat over the Yuma TACTS Range.

stall in an extremely high angle of attack, with one wing low and maybe the flame-out of one engine due to lack of airflow, its crew can find itself in deep kim chi. The F-4 is infamous for flopping onto its back and entering a flat inverted spin from which there is no recovery. The Tomcat is somewhat more tractable in a similar situation, but several have been lost in departure spins. Navy fighter pilots now undergo recurrent stall-spin training in forgiving T-2 Buckeyes to prepare them for this risky eventuality.

At the end of the brief for each Top Gun flight, one pilot for each plane in the hop will be called upon to recite from memory the standard NATOPS departure drill for his aircraft. It pours out in an effortless and obviously ingrained blur

Filming for *Top Gun* at NAS Fallon brought dogfighting down to, and occasionally below, mountaintop level. Here "Maverick" and "Goose" ruin "Jester's" whole day.

of words: "Stick forward, neutral lateral, lock harness. Rudder opposite turn needles or yaw. If no recovery, stick into direction of spin. If engine stalls, throttles to idle. If recovery indicated, neutralize controls and recover at seventeen units angle of attack. If spin confirmed due to flat attitude, increasing yaw rate, eyeballs-out G, lack of pitch and roll rate—jettison canopy and RIO will command eject prior to 10,000 feet AGL." Thus goes the F-14 drill.

Most Top Gun engagements honor a 10,000-foot "hard deck" to allow room for maneuver, and ejection, if one of the players should "drop off." A school F-5 was lost in such an incident in 1984; several other departures have had happier endings. Top Gun instructor Greg "Hollywood" Dishart actually rewrote the official departure drill for the F-5 while on the hot seat. Finding himself in a flat spin at 22,000 feet after a furious attempt to go vertical in a 1 V 1, he ran through the thoroughly memorized departure drill without result. Plummeting through 10,000 feet—time to step outside—he resignedly tried one last trick: full opposite rudder, a procedure not called for in the drill. The little jet cheerfully dropped its nose, and Dishart pulled out with several thousand feet to spare. "Our F-5s have turn needles, and the Air Force birds don't. That leaves them without a good way to determine spin direction, so their drill says to give it up when you're upside down. We've added 'rudder opposite turn needles' to our procedure. Worked for me." The low point of the experience, recalls Hollywood, was his merciless Marine opponent (don't worry, Tiny, I won't name names) calling a "Fox Two" (Sidewinder) shot on him as he spiraled earthward! War is indeed hell.

There's far too much performance information to memorize. Every knot of speed, every tiny change in power setting, every foot of altitude, every degree of bank or angle of attack, every increase in G-loading will alter a jet's moves. Ultimately the pilot must rely on his skill and experience to keep his airplane at the ragged edge of its capability. Most fighters will telegraph their distress via stick-shakes and other variations of the funky chicken as they approach the black hole of departure. These signals are hard to describe, but they're a bit like the sound of a rattlesnake—the first time you encounter it, you somehow know what it is. The new computer-controlled fly-by-wire jets, like the F-16, the F-18, and the Mirage 2000, have self-diagnosing departure software integrated into the control systems. Their departure drills could hardly be simpler: lock your harness, then let loose of the stick and allow the black boxes to solve the recovery problem.

Knowing the outer limits of one's own fighter is only half the battle. The real key to winning is knowing and anticipating the other guy's moves as well. Top Gun instructors are adept at flying their jets in imitation of potential threats. The A-4 Mongoose can turn and zoom just like the earlier Mirages. The F-5 can do without its maneuvering flaps to mimic the ubiquitous MiG-21 Fishbed. The newer MiG-23 Flogger is easy for the F-5 to simulate: go like a bullet, and turn like one. When the F-16N arrives in 1987, Top Gun will at last be able to launch a sparring partner that can fly ACM right up to the capabilities of just about any fighter in the world.

Top Gun has devised a simple category system, I through IV, into which it lumps every known threat in the air. Category I represents the minimum threat—old propeller fighters and the like, while Category IV encompasses the fourth generation—the U.S. teen fighters, the NATO Tornado, the Mirage 2000, the Russian RAM-jets. A given fight may put a student up against, say, a Category III bogey with rear-quarter missiles and guns, for which read MiG-21, Atoll missiles, 23mm cannon.

Ideally the fighter pilot will want to know a lot more than that. He'll try to determine whether his bogey is heavy or light on gas and weapons. A lightweight fighter with relatively small engines, like the F-5, will turn into a little pig with full fuel and an extra center-line tank. Often Top Gun

instructors will fly engagements with two different fighters on a single hop, and the sharp student will learn to tailor his tactics accordingly: fight one way on the first bounce (instructor heavy) and another way on the second (instructor light). With an actual enemy, of course, there is no real way to be sure of his fuel and weapons state until he shows his colors and moves at the merge. And as the fight progresses, he'll reveal something far

"Hollywood" Dishart returns plane captain's salute before rolling his F-5 for a 1 V 1 engagement.

LT. DISHART
HOLLYWOOD

more important—the degree of skill and aggressiveness in his own head and heart.

It is fitting to close this chapter with a look at a fight that remains the most epic 1 V 1 in the history of naval aviation. It was a battle between two widely different aircraft, each flown beyond the hundredth percentile by a superb air combat tactician. Lt. (now commander and skipper of Adversary squadron VF-126) Randy "Duke" Cunningham, flying a Phantom with VF-96 off the carrier *Constellation*, was returning from a flak suppression mission over Haiphong, North Vietnam; the date was 10 May 1972. In Cunningham's back seat was RIO Willie Driscoll. A huge air battle had developed over the target and Cunningham and Driscoll, separated from their wingman, were disengaging from this furball and heading for the boat after having bagged two MiGs with one Sidewinder apiece.

Approaching the coast at 10,000 feet, Duke spotted a Gomer MiG-17 closing nose-on. Duke angled for a close pass, so as to limit his opponent's ability to turn onto his six. First mistake: the aggressive bogey's nose lit up as he dropped the hammer on his 23mm cannons. Unbeknownst to Cunningham and Driscoll, they had come up against the mysterious and shadowy "Colonel Toon," supposedly the war's premiere ace with thirteen American kills to his credit. In retrospect it is likely that Toon was a propaganda amalgam of several fine Communist pilots, but regardless of specific identity it is obvious that the Phantom crew was tussling with as fine a dogfighter as the enemy had produced.

Duke reefed the huge Phantom into six Gs vertical pullup, sure of his ability to separate from the weaker Fresco. He anticipated a half-hearted horizontal turn, if not a bug-out, and he planned a diving Sidewinder attack from the top of his zoom climb. Looking over his ejection seat for a glimmer of the enemy, he was chilled and astonished to see an impossible sight; the MiG-17 was barely one hundred yards away, climbing canopy to canopy, its pilot regarding him calmly from behind World-War-II-style goggles. Duke lit the burners, knowing he could accelerate away from the little single-engine fighter. Second mistake: pulling away in the vertical presented his six to the enemy's guns. Shit flew. Duke rolled desperately off the top and spiraled downward, Toon following and firing. The two adversaries entered a classic rolling scissors, each straining for angles on the other. The series of tight turns dragged the Phantom down toward two hundred knots, where the little MiG enjoyed vastly superior turning and handling properties.

Duke managed to break free and run downhill for two miles of separation. With energy and momentum restored, he nosed back into the MiG and blasted into sixty degrees of vertical. Again, the Fresco snap-turned and climbed after the Phantom. Such vertical tactics were thought to be beyond the capabilities of the old Russian fighter, but no one had told Toon. It was a repeat of the first engagement, Duke dropping out of the vertical with the Vietnamese firing from beneath, the two jets again entering a rolling scissors as both adversaries strained for angles. As the Phantom again slowed from the regimen of tight turns, an enraged Cunningham yanked the bird out of the fight and roared away in a descending dash to regain energy. He was determined to seize the offensive, which had rested with the Communist ace since the first pass.

Once again Cunningham and Driscoll met the MiG-17 head-on, this time with a slight offset so

Toon couldn't use his cannons. As they passed again and headed into the vertical, Duke played his trump—he pulled into Toon, dragged the throttles to idle, and popped his "boards," or speed brakes. The Phantom, sixty degrees nose-up, dropped below 150 knots airspeed, and Duke had to slam the engines into burner to stay in the sky. The surprised enemy couldn't react in time to keep from shooting out in front. The quick-thinking Toon pitched back and dropped straight down, knowing that the Phantom could follow but feeling confident that the heat-seeking Sidewinder would be flustered by ground clutter if the American took his shot.

Cunningham had the same concern, but he unleashed the third of his four AIM-9s regardless. To his dismay, it appeared to miss. Just as he tightened his finger to fire his last missile, the MiG-17 spewed flame and dense black smoke. It flew straight into the ground, at a forty-degree angle, seemingly in control. There was no ejection. The victory was the fifth and last for Cunningham and Driscoll; their valiant bird was hit by a SAM as it approached the North Vietnamese coast. Duke and Willie ejected safely into the South China Sea after nursing the burning jet past the coastline. Both aces had learned their lessons well as students in the Navy's first Top Gun class.

---

10 May 1972: Randy "Duke" Cunningham, flying with RIO Willie Driscoll in CAG-9's "double nuts" F-4, heads Downtown with ACM loadout of two Sparrows, four Sidewinders. Both became aces on this date, killing three MiGs with AIM-9 missiles.

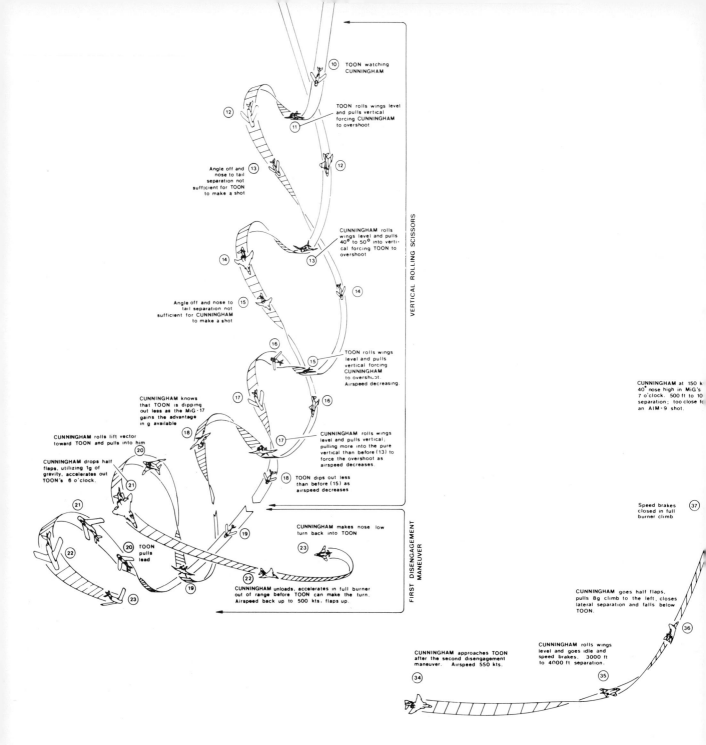

10 TOON watching CUNNINGHAM

TOON rolls wings level and pulls vertical forcing CUNNINGHAM to overshoot

Angle off and nose to tail separation not sufficient for TOON to make a shot

CUNNINGHAM rolls wings level and pulls 40° to 50° into vertical forcing TOON to overshoot

Angle off and nose to tail separation not sufficient for CUNNINGHAM to make a shot

TOON rolls wings level and pulls vertical forcing CUNNINGHAM to overshoot. Airspeed decreasing.

CUNNINGHAM knows that TOON is dipping out less as the MiG-17 gains the advantage in g available

CUNNINGHAM rolls lift vector toward TOON and pulls into him

CUNNINGHAM drops half flaps, utilizing 1g of gravity, accelerates out TOON's 6 o'clock.

CUNNINGHAM rolls wings level and pulls vertical; pulling more into the pure vertical than before (13) to force the overshoot as airspeed decreases.

TOON dips out less than before (15) as airspeed decreases

VERTICAL ROLLING SCISSORS

CUNNINGHAM at 150 k... 40° nose high in MiG's 7 o'clock. 500 ft to 10... separation; too close fo... an AIM-9 shot.

Speed brakes closed in full burner climb

FIRST DISENGAGEMENT MANEUVER

CUNNINGHAM makes nose low turn back into TOON

TOON pulls lead

CUNNINGHAM unloads, accelerates in full burner out of range before TOON can make the turn. Airspeed back up to 500 kts, flaps up.

CUNNINGHAM goes half flaps, pulls 8g climb to the left, closes lateral separation and falls below TOON.

CUNNINGHAM approaches TOON after the second disengagement maneuver. Airspeed 550 kts.

CUNNINGHAM rolls wings level and goes idle and speed brakes. 3000 ft to 4000 ft separation.

78

"Duel of the Aces": a graphic representation of the epic Cunningham-Toon dogfight, 10 May 1972. (Special thanks to matchless aviation illustrators Matt and Mark Waki for permission to reproduce portions of "Duel.")

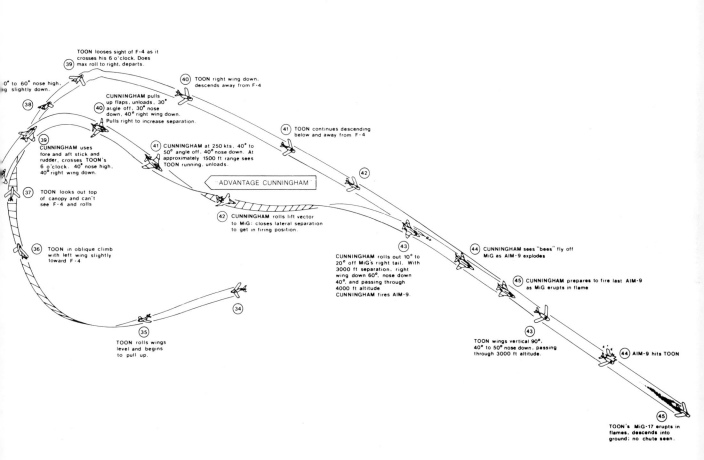

Section Tactics

Dogfighting 1 V 1 may be the essence of air combat, but the likely reality is far different. Modern fighter pilots will have to anticipate and be prepared to defeat multi-plane enemy forces arrayed at widely varying ranges off the nose. Navy pilots in particular must expect to face greatly superior numbers since the Soviets, and the many surrogate air forces they supply and train, like to rely on lots and lots of airplanes.

Carrier pilots won't have that luxury. The typical carrier battle group will field about twenty-four F-14s and another twenty-four F-18s that share fighter and attack duties. Bring in another battle group and double those numbers—a routine possibility in the Mediterranean—and the good guys will still have a hard time putting up sixty fighters. Third-rate sandlots like Libya and Syria can launch five times that number if they get mad enough. The only reliable plan is to jump in with aircraft, pilots, ordnance and tactics that are at least five times better.

Top Gun students start thinking and flying multi-plane tactics in the second week of the Power Projection course. Students are set up into two-fighter sections; these pairs fly MiG sweep and MiGCAP (combat air patrol) missions over both desert and ocean practice areas. The Top Gun instructors gang up with the adversary pilots who sit in on the first three weeks of the class, and these bogeys spar with the students in varying combinations of 2 V 1, 2 V 2, 2 V 4, or 2 V many/

Previous spread: Fleet defense: Student F-14s roll into surprise attack on three-ship of Top Gun Skyhawks.

unknown. Combat air controllers on the ground vector the combatants toward each other, the F-14 and F-18 crews also utilizing their on-board radar to effect the merge.

There is no assurance, of course, that the bad guys will conveniently show up off the nose, drenched in electrons from the powerful Hughes radars in the Hornets and Tomcats. In fact it's a good bet that they won't, and the students will have to keep their eyes behind the three-nine line as well as on the radar screen. The ground controllers might call the bogeys in the rear quarter, and then again they might not. The students' work load shoots way up in these multi-plane hops.

The student crews are sometimes paired off arbitrarily into sections, but Marine F-18 drivers, who are often sent to Top Gun in pairs from the same squadron, naturally hook up with each other in the second week. Having had experience flying wing with one another can be a big advantage. In a tradition born of necessity in World War I, pilots flying section or division tactics work out contracts with each other, dividing responsibilities and committing various procedures to formality.

The contract is utterly central to multi-plane ACM tactics. Michael Skinner writes in *USAFE: A Primer of Modern Air Combat in Europe*:

The contract is never written down, but it is more binding than anything the pilot will ever sign. The penalty for not fulfilling the contract is to be branded a Whiskey Delta, a "weak dick," with all the personal and professional demerits that implies. In wartime, the consequences of a broken contract are even more severe—the death of one, or both, pilots.

Skinner was speaking of Air Force F-15 pilots in this case, but the existence of the contract is universal in the fighter world. Bet on the Boys In

Red relying on their contracts too. They'd be fools not to.

The contract is a verbal agreement between pilot and wingman, and between the front and back seat of the Tomcat and other multi-crew birds. The idea is to *know* what your buddy is going to do, particularly in a fight or an emergency. The middle of a 500-knot furball is not the place to initiate a discussion of appropriate tactics on the radio. Besides, the Soviets and their pals are big on communications jamming; believe it or not, a powerful jammer can make it impossible for two planes to talk on the radio even when they're only a wingspan apart.

The contract will cover things like code words and procedures. As one small example, once the canopy is closed on an F-14, neither pilot nor RIO will ever utter the word "eject" in any context unless he means EJECT. Most RIOs have a con-

"Students" and "instructors" form up for Clay Lacy's photo Learjet during filming of *Top Gun* at NAS Fallon, Nevada.

tractual understanding with their pilots that although they have the capability to light the Sparrow and Phoenix long-range missiles from the back seat (only the pilot has control over the Sidewinders and the gun), they will only call the shots—the pilot will squeeze them off.

Sections of single-seat jets will have a sky-scanning plan figured out: if flying line abreast, each pilot will take the outside hemisphere, or perhaps one will look up and one down. Tomcat crews also divide up eyeball duties, usually front to back. Maneuvers and formations are covered in the contract, so each pilot will know what to do if one or the other (or both!) gets bounced. A loose deuce pair of fighters may contract for a defensive split if jumped by a single bogey: one will make a sharp horizontal turn and the other will pull vertical, leaving the bad guy with an angles-or-energy choice. A weak fighter might feel forced to take the horizontal opportunity; the climbing jet will then switch back and drop down for a shot. If the Gomer goes for the vertical, the turning fighter will reverse and climb after him, waiting for his wingman to separate at the top of the arc before firing his missile. Like so many section maneuvers, it takes nerve, timing, and complete confidence in each other. An experienced section will be able to make it work without so much as a single word on the radio.

The 2 V 2 scenario is more common in Top Gun's second week. But leave it to the instructors

Facing page: Pilot's eye viewpoint, as well as the overview from above, can be recreated in real time on TACTS (Tactical Aircrew Combat Training System) for review and debrief of aerial engagements.

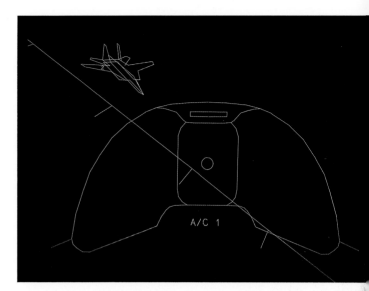

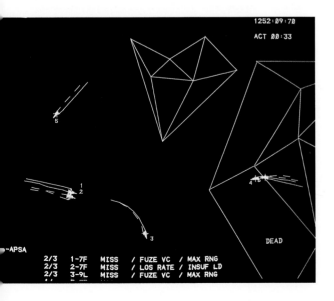

1252:09:70
ACT 00:33

DEAD

-APSA
2/3   1-7F   MISS   / FUZE VC   / MAX RNG
2/3   2-7F   MISS   / LOS RATE / INSUF LD
2/3   3-9L   MISS   / FUZE VC   / MAX RNG

to throw in a wild card in the form of a third bogey tagging along a couple of miles behind a tightly welded two-ship of F-5s or A-4s. McCudden and von Richtofen liked this simple trick in World War I. So did Colonel Toon, who hung around as a fifth to the common North Vietnamese four-ship flight. It was an unpredictable maneuver, and it helped him arrange fatal surprises for thirteen American aircrews. Ironically, it was Cunningham's unpredictable maneuver—dropping the anchor in the vertical—that surprised Toon into a fatal overshoot. It's one of Top Gun's unwritten but most important lessons: lie, cheat, and steal in the cockpit. Leave chivalry hanging in the closet with your dress whites.

Speaking of lying and cheating, for decades the rule in the mock dogfight was that the first man back to the officers' club bar was the winner, if only because he would get to tell his side first. Top Gun hops from the second week onward make use of an amazing electronic system that threatens to end forever the spectacle of grown fighter pilots pointing fingers and saying I-got-you-no-I-got-you-first. The system is called TACTS (Tactical Aircrew Combat Training System), and yes, it really exists. Many viewers who saw the system featured in the movie *Top Gun* assumed it to be a fanciful invention of George Lucas's special effects boys. TACTS is made up of a grid of data

Feel the need for speed! Tomcat blasts along the desert floor at the speed of heat. Low-level work in the later weeks of the Top Gun syllabus can be a real eye-opener for interceptor pilots used to high altitudes.

sensors spread around the desert ranges west of Yuma, Arizona; a couple of very powerful computers; small data transmitters mounted on the Sidewinder rails of the competing airplanes; and microwave-linked control positions, with rows of theater seats and large viewing screens, at both MCAS Yuma and Miramar. TACTS permits pilots and others to view an ACM engagement in real-time computer simulation from various viewpoints—through the combatants' windshields, from one plane to another, or from a "God's-eye" perspective. Pertinent data from the fighters' HUDs are also displayed, along with a clock that times the moves to the millisecond.

Top Gun jocks (and lots of other fighter types based around southern California) duke it out over the Yuma range and then set down at Yuma or Miramar for far more sophisticated and precise debriefs than were ever possible before. TACTS is a cosmic umpire, and there is no appeal from its verdicts. Top Gun instructors supplement the TACTS data with comments recorded on small cassette machines; with practice, they can reconstruct a complex fight almost as accurately as the computers. They also shoot film with 16mm gun cameras, largely to critique last-ditch guns defense maneuvers. Most F-18s and the newer F-14s carry TV cameras and videotape recorders that watch the fight through the HUD for later playback.

The TACTS range gets a partial rest in the middle of the third week of instruction, as half the class now switches to division tactics, flying hops with four and more planes on each side. The division exercises are another quantum jump in complexity over the 2 V unknowns of the previous week. Not only are there a whole lot of airplanes in the sky, but realistic threat factors start to enter

Above: Marine F-4 slips past Mach-1 in a particularly frantic multi-plane engagement. *Below:* Hornet pilot's HUD view of a guns kill on his hapless wingman.

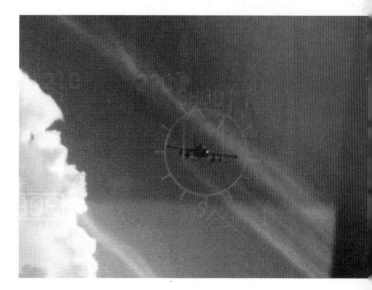

the picture. These flights stage out of MCAS Yuma, a large tactical Marine base one hundred miles east of Miramar. From Yuma the flight heads north to a corner of the vast China Lake Naval Weapons Test Center, a desert base situated roughly between Edwards AFB and Death Valley.

China Lake's "Echo Range" adds a chilling element to Top Gun training. On the ground, sweltering in the desert's usual three-digit temperatures, is a platoon of highly trained threat operators who employ all manner of electronic trickery to simulate ground-to-air threats — surface-to-air missiles, radar-controlled "triple-A" (anti-aircraft guns like the Soviet ZSU-23-4 "Zip Gun"), radar and com jamming. As if the students don't have enough to worry about, what with instructors and adversary pilots coming at them from all sides, they now have to pay attention as well to the various bells and whistles that alert them to the tracking efforts of the ground threats. The threat boys send shot analyses and ground-camera videotapes down to Top Gun, showing some pretty ugly tracking solutions on the attacking aircraft. Some of the third-week debriefs can be a bit demoralizing for the students.

The hard deck works its way down to five hundred feet AGL over Echo Range; getting low and masking the aircraft behind terrain features is usually the best way to penetrate a dense SAM/AAA belt. But it's an eye-opener for the jet driv-

Facing page: Top Gun skipper Comdr. Rick "Wigs" Ludwig poses with his F-5E after a session over the Yuma TACTS Range.

Low-level attack craft like the AH-64 Apache (*above*) and the A-10 Thunderbolt (*below*) can be dead meat for a canny fighter pilot, unless the mud-movers can bring the fight around to their own terms.

Tomcat student effectively uses terrain-masking in a low-level fight over the NAS Fallon range.

ers; the world moves by awfully fast at five hundred knots and five hundred feet, and the margin for error drops to sub-zero. Top Gun has managed to keep its accident rate remarkably low over its seventeen-year history, thanks to a combination of skill, extreme safety consciousness, and spectacular good luck. The huge Red Flag exercises, held quarterly over the nearby Nellis AFB ranges and involving similar low-level practice missions, have had a much worse time of it, particularly in the early years; some fifty aircraft have crashed during Red Flags, and forty aviators have died.

Some other strange and wonderful threats can be found lurking in the weeds. High-flying fighter jocks aren't terribly comfortable down in the dirt, but another bunch of tactical pilots, the close-air support specialists, are in their element. Mud moving aircraft like the A-10 Thunderbolt (uni-versally known as the "Warthog" among fans and detractors alike) and hot attack helicopters like the Army's new AH-64 Apache can deal harshly with the hottest fighters if they can pull them down onto the deck. No one would claim that the A-10, for instance, is a true ACM fighter; it's much too slow — scarcely faster than the hot helos — and its thrust-to-weight ratio is rock bottom. But its huge straight wing and flaps give it matchless snap-turn capabilities, and its tortoise-like pace could easily cause a fighter pilot to overshoot in a bounce. A fighter that hurtles ahead of the Hog's three-nine line will have to give some thought to his principal armament—a 30mm antitank cannon the size of a Japanese car, rapid-firing bullets as big as milk bottles. A single round will take out anything that flies. The attack helos have smaller Gatling guns, and most can be configured to carry all-aspect Sidewinders. Of course the Soviets, those lovable imitators, have their own operational versions of the A-10 and the Apache. Trying to go down, slow down and turn with any of these characters would be a drastic mistake for any fighter—the deadly error of playing by his rules instead of yours.

Weeks three and four of the Power Projection course contain some other interesting experiences for Fleet and Marine fighter drivers. A recent addition to the curriculum, in response to hundreds of very real encounters in the Mediterranean, is a "line of death" or Gulf of Sidra escort mission. Instructors and adversaries, simulating

Air Force 64th Aggressors, flying F-5s, serve as guest Gomers in the later weeks of the Top Gun curriculum.

E-2 Hawkeye provides carrier-based airborne command-and-control of the fight in the air. Three controllers handle various aspects of the battle via radar, voice com, and data links.

Libyan MiGs, Fitters and Mirages, will sidle up to the students who are playing the fighter-escort role. Unlike other Top Gun intercepts, there is no assurance that a fight will result—that is the object lesson. Much as the typical Navy or Marine fighter pilot would delight in popping one of his Libyan counterparts, he can not do so unless true hostile intent has been demonstrated. There have in fact been almost four hundred intercepts over the past few years around battle groups in the southern Med, and only one has resulted in Sidewinders being turned loose. The Top Gun students get some practice in gauging the bad guys' intentions, watching for subtle moves, and above all keeping behind the Gomers' wing lines.

When the students have moved through two-thirds of the course, their ACM skills have shot up like a Lorenz curve, and the instructors find themselves scraping the bottom of their trick bags. Time to arrange a couple of exhibition hops with another bunch of shit-hot dogfighters, the 64th

and 65th Aggressor squadrons out of Nellis AFB near Las Vegas. These guys, also flying Soviet-camouflaged F-5s, are the Top Gun instructors' Air Force counterparts; they're no better at dog-fighting, but neither are they any worse. They're bound to be just a bit different, though, and they usually have a couple of new gimmicks to spring on the Top Gun students. Several Top Gun teachers are regularly detailed for varying periods to hold down "guest professorships" with the Aggressors and, next door on the Nellis flight line, the Air Force Fighter Weapons School.

Week four winds up with more low-level work on Echo Range and several hops involving forward-quarter tactics with all three air-to-air missiles. Much as the Top Gun staffers wanted to cooperate with me in the preparation of this book, they tended to look at the ceiling and count holes in the acoustical tile when I pressed them for details on missile envelopes and nose-to-nose tactics. It's top-secret stuff, with hardware, software, and tactics in constant flux. Suffice it to say, without going into classified detail, the three missiles with their overlapping ranges are working extremely well these days, and even the balky Sparrow, a disappointing performer for so long, has finally been whipped into line. It's fair to assume that these hops encompass differing rules of engagement related to IFF (Identification of Friend or Foe) at ranges beyond eyesight.

The Tomcat and Phantom RIOs come into their own in these more complex week-three and week-four missions. In the first hops, the RIOs are little more than a second pair of eyes, although that's nothing to sneeze at. The *Top Gun* director and writers, with a lot of guidance from the school staff, did an excellent job of getting across the importance of constant visual contact. One of the film's most enduring images is that of back-seater

Instructors in F-5F (*left*) and A-4 Mongoose (*right*) form up with a VF-302 Tomcat after a friendly fight over China Lake.

"Goose" grabbing the ACM handle and swiveling against the G-forces to eyeball the bad guys. Navy fliers call it "doing the Linda Blair," referring to the possessed prepubescent in the movie *The Exorcist* and her ability (which any RIO would kill for) to rotate her head 360 degrees.

In the multi-plane hops, with long-range intercepts and instructions from ground controllers, the RIOs spend less time scanning the heavens and more time with their heads buried in the radar scopes. It's in the radar intercept that the F-4 and F-14 become true two-man airplanes. Their powerful but older-generation analog radars require a lot of tweaking, interpreting, and knob twisting, and RIOs vary widely in their ability to make the radar talk. The best RIOs can psych out the enemy's moves and figure out the fight well before the merge. There's a saying in the Tomcat community, "As goes the intercept, so goes the engagement."

Although many old-line fighter pilots (particularly those in the Air Force F-15 world) swear by the single-seat fighter, the fact is that the work

Student and teacher head for the landing break over Yuma. Tomcat tailspan is actually larger than the tiny Tiger's wingspan.

load soars to 110 percent in the multi-plane intercept scenario. The superb digital radar in the F-18 is designed for ease of one-man operation, but there is a growing coterie of lobbyists for a two-seat version of the Hornet with uprated powerplants. In fact, the Marines are moving towards a fifty–fifty mix of one- and two-seat Hornets in all of their squadrons. The two-seaters will be primarily attack bombers, but the planes will be entirely ACM-capable as well. It is perhaps revealing that almost all of Israel's F-16s are set up as dual-role two-seaters.

The last week at Top Gun is a mixture of large-scale strike missions and a few wild cards. A favorite hop is called the graduation 1 V 1. After weeks of section and division work, the staff throws one last 1 V 1 party, and it's a doozy. Guest Gomers of all stripes are invited to fly to Yuma and jump in; past baddies have included Air Force teen jets, low-level attack birds seldom encountered in dogfights, and just about anyone else who can be talked into fighting—the weirder, the better. Only the exercise coordinator knows who will fight whom; students might draw Top Gun pilots, fellow students or one of the mystery guests. Each

---

Nasty letters of challenge fire up the combatants for the graduation 1 V 1 hops. No one other than the exercise coordinator knows who will draw whom in the fights.

Yankee Imperialist dog,

It has come to the attention of the Motherland that you are, how do you say, KING KONG amongst your apple-pie-eating colleagues. We therefore challenge you to meet our Hero of The Socialist Peoples in area _PAPA 1_ at _1245_ to engage in a one-versus-one battle calculated to demonstrate to you the overwhelming superiority of our system. We look forward, after our bullets have ventilated your cockpit, to relaxing by sipping Margaritas along your coastline, your lovely wives and girlfriends as our companions. LONG LIVE GLORIOUS SOCIALISM!

Yours in revolution,

Mick

Mikhail S. Gorbachev

Your call sign: _GOON 16_
Our call sign: _GOON 24_

Your Cap Station: _P-1N_
Our Cap Station: _P-15_

Your controller: _CHARLES MANSON_
Frequency: _384.5_

You are a __1__ shot kill if fired upon by a forward quarter missile.

Dear Communist FAGGOT,

So you want to join us for a little bumping, huh? Nothing would please us more than to take to the skies, toy with your inept abilities, and obliterate your pitiful, obsolete machinery.

We accept your ill-advised challenge to meet your spoob-eating representative in area _PAPA 1_ at _1245_ to engage in a one-versus-one engagement, to show you the terminal hopelessness of your folly. Rest in peace, young Communist, with the thought that our matchless young aviators are looking forward to taking a dump on your grave and ravishing your lovely women face-down on the parade ground!

Truth, Justice, And The American Way!

Ron

Ronnie Reagan

Your call sign: _GOON 24_
Our call sign: _GOON 16_

Your Cap Station: _P-15_
Our Cap Station: _P-1N_

Your controller: _CHARLES MANSON_
Frequency: _384.5_

You are a __1__ shot kill, forward quarter.

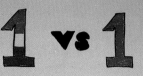

player is handed a sealed letter which includes some insulting prose ("Dear Communist Pig," "Esteemed Imperialist Lackey") and a time, location and radio frequency for the single joust.

Students and teachers gather in Classroom 1 for a rah-rah mass brief, and all are advised to keep an eye out for strange and wondrous opponents. Just before the envelopes are handed out, Top Gun instructors are called upon to recite departure drills for an oddball collection of adversaries—MiG-21, F-106, F-20, British Sepecat Jaguar, even hoary World War II numbers like the F-4U Corsair (Sandy "Jaws" Winnefeld holding forth on the latter: "...cowl flaps open, prop pitch full forward..."). Graduate 1 V 1 coordinators have even been nagging Flight Systems, a civilian outfit that flies retired military jets in ordnance testing and target towing missions, to send down one of their Canadian-built F-86 Sabres to take part. Talk about MiG-17 simulators!

Left: Instructor Willie "Tex" Spence whips the whole class, plus guest baddies, into a frenzy for the graduation 1 V 1 fights. *Right:* A bit of 1 V 1 doggerel, with apologies to Thomas à Becket.

One tradition is vigorously enforced after the fights: the victors get to suck up into a tight echelon leading to an ultra-snappy break over the field, while the vanquished must fly an ignominious straight-in instrument approach via the despised Poway TACAN. It's just about the only moment in the Top Gun course when horn tooting is encouraged.

The course winds up with two huge strike

Facing page: Top Gun F-5F RIO and A-4 Mongoose await takeoff clearance at the end of Miramar's busy runways.

packages that hopefully encompass everything learned in the five weeks. One is an all-out fighter battle with the class and instructors meeting in an epic merge. The final hop is called the "graduation coordinated strike"; it is a huge logistical exercise involving the whole class, the whole staff, and guest assets ranging from A-6 and A-7 strike bombers to tankers, ELINT jammers, E-2 Hawkeyes, and just about anyone else who wants to join in an attack on Echo Range. Then it's all over except for an exhaustive six-hour student critique of the course, a graduation ceremony, and a revolting Thursday night class party, about which the less said the better. No sense in alarming the wives and girlfriends waiting back home for their fearless sky warriors.

No dissertation on present-day section tactics, or on naval aviation in general, could be considered complete without a brace of "Hoser" stories. In a microworld of perhaps 400 Tomcat pilots, a few legendary gonzo maniacs are going to bubble to the surface. Joe "Hoser" Satrapa was already famous in Vietnam as a young and utterly fearless F-8 pilot who regularly carried a good forty pounds of lethal ordnance — leaning toward small automatic weapons and hand grenades — in case he was suddenly compelled to leave his aircraft and carry the battle directly to the little bad guys in the jungle.

Guns were Hoser's game in the air; he flew the four-gun Crusader — which many Navy pilots still regard as the tits machine of all time — in Southeast Asia, and he'd never been forced to rely totally on missiles like his Navy Phantom cohorts. After negotiations that would shame the pro football draft, Hoser was dragooned back into the Tomcat front seat as a RAG guns instructor. This, after personal entreaties from the highest levels up to and including Secretary of the Navy John Lehman, himself a Reserve naval aviator.

Many active pilots and RIOs well remember Hoser's delivery of manic harangues to fuzzy-cheeked newcomers from the RAG. In his patented Yosemite Sam voice he would whip the lads, and invariably himself, into a lethal frenzy: "Pull on the pole till the rivets pop and the RIO pukes! No kill like a guns kill! A Lima up the tailpipe is too good for any Gomer! Close with the miserable Commie bastard and put a few rounds of twenty-mike-mike through his goddam canopy! If he hits the silk, gun his ass while he swings!" Hoser would then pace the corridor, bumping into hapless petty officers, muttering oaths, trying to realign his internal INS.

Hoser also knew a thing or two about the element of surprise. During the much-maligned AIMVAL-ACEVAL fighter trials a decade ago, Hoser was put up in a 1 V 1 against a Navy Aggressor flying an F-5. As the two combatants sat side-by-side on the Nellis runway, awaiting tower clearance for a section takeoff, Hoser looked over at his opponent, reached his hands up over the panel, and mimicked the cocking of machine guns in a World War I Spad. A thumbs up came from the other cockpit — guns it would be, the proverbial knife fight in a phone booth, forget the missiles. Both jets blasted off.

In the area, the fighters set up twenty miles apart for a head-on intercept under ground control. Seven miles from the merge, with closure well over 1000 knots, Hoser called "Fox One" — Sparrow missile away, no chance of a miss. As they flashed past each other, the furious F-5 driver radioed, "What the hell was that all about?" "Sorry," said Hoser, "lost my head. Let's set up again. Guns only. I promise."

Remember Charlie Brown, Lucy, and the football? Again the two fighters streaked toward the pass, again at seven miles Hoser called "Fox One." The Aggressor was apoplectic; he was also coming up on bingo fuel state, a common situation in the short-legged F-5.

Hoser was first back to the club bar, nursing an end-of-the-day cold one as the flushed Aggressor stomped in. "Hoser, what the hell happened to credibility?" fumed the F-5 jock. Said Hoser, with accompanying thumb gestures, "Credibility is DOWN, kill ratio is UP!" It's a popular Top Gun story, and its moral isn't lost on students or teachers. From 1 V 1 to forty-plane furball, expect anything. But *never* expect your enemy to be a sweet guy.

Scale models represent virtually every American, Allied, Neutral, and Gomer jet a Top Gun student is likely to encounter in a fight.

Knock It Off

"Fight's on" is the clarion call for the military dogfighter, and "knock it off" is the standard cease-fire phrase; wings roll level, adrenalin ebbs, and glint-eyed adversaries form up in fingertip echelon for the all-important class pass over the flight line. Top Gun jousts are invariably followed by debriefs at Miramar or Yuma that can take twenty times as long as the fights themselves.

Before heading into the briefing room, pilots make a quick stop at the maintenance desk to report any problems, or "gripes," that need attention before the planes go up again. Top Gun's A-4s are cared for by enlisted Navy personnel, and the F-5s are maintained by civilians working for Northrop, their manufacturer. The A-4s are among the oldest airplanes in the Navy, and the F-5s go them one better—the Top Gun Tigers are the world's high-time F-5s, with several approaching 5,000 airframe hours. Most of those hours have been spent in the worst kind of flying a military jet can endure—all-out air combat, with maximum G-loadings and constant changes in engine power settings. The Top Gun line crews, civilian and military, do a magnificent job with their tired little scooters; mission-ready rates are right up on par with most Navy squadrons. But it gets harder and harder to keep them flying, and the new F-16s can't show up too soon. Said former Top Gun skipper Comdr. Ernie "Ratchet" Christensen, "I flew the Skyhawk in Vietnam in 1966, and it was old then. It's not any newer now."

Previous spread: Gaggle of students and instructors form up for the all-important bad-to-the-bone break over the Miramar runway. The fighter pilot's credo: Look good, whatever the cost.

At Top Gun the debrief is fully as important as the fight. The school stresses teaching and learning far more than winning and losing, and the briefs are the principal vehicles for one-on-one instruction. Fighter pilots are by nature aggressive, competitive, egotistical, and a bit hard to teach. Top Gun instructors must have parallel skills; they have to be better than the best in the air, but they must also be tactful and seemingly devoid of ego or self-aggrandizement. A shit-hot Tomcat pilot who has just been hosed repeatedly by a thirty-year-old A-4 has to be taught what he did wrong, not ridiculed or humiliated. Instructors try to keep things upbeat in the debriefs, mixing in lots of attaboys to counterbalance the negative comments. There is no "I" or "you" in a

Simple F-5s lack ground intercoms, so crewmen use hand signals to convey preflight info.

Top Gun debrief: it's always "the Tomcat" or "the F-5."

Probably the most glaring error in the *Top Gun* movie was the exaggeration of student-teacher and student-student competitiveness. There is no class champ, no perpetual trophy; Top Gun goes to considerable pains to play down this type of teeth gnashing. Hostile and dangerous vendettas between pupil and teacher are unheard-of. And forget those madcap, boys-will-be-boys antics like buzzing the tower at a hundred feet. Navy pilots have lost their wings for a lot less.

Of course the worm soon turns, and by mid-course it's the teachers who are getting hosed. It takes a special kind of fighter pilot to enjoy getting beat, but the Top Gun teachers actually get a kick out of watching the students improve their skills. "You bounce a guy and he pulls a sharp defensive maneuver; then all of a sudden he's offensive,

Top Gun Tigers sport various Warsaw Pact and Middle Eastern camouflage paint schemes, the better to confuse students used to dogfighting with larger, similarly painted jets.

Navy enlisted men (and women) do a larger-than-life job of maintaining Top Gun's ancient Skyhawks, some of the highest-time jets in the entire Navy inventory. Northrop contract civilians care for the equally aged F-5s.

showing up on your six," says an instructor. "Two weeks ago he didn't know how to do that. You're damn right it's satisfying."

The Top Gun graduates are destined to become teachers themselves; a chosen few will return to the NFWS staff, but all are expected to pass along their new-found knowledge when they return to their units. The class sits through an excellent lecture on teaching techniques with an emphasis on instruction in a squadron setting. Sometimes the new grads have a tough job; there is often sour-grapes resentment among other junior pilots who weren't chosen for the school, and old hands might be disinclined to learn new tricks from the newly ordained hotshots. There have also been instances of squadron commanders, unimpressed with Top Gun for one reason or another, burying graduates in irrelevant staff jobs where they can't pass on what they've learned.

But these are isolated examples. Most squadron-mates are anxious to pick up on the latest

Top Gun skipper's F-5E sports experimental camouflage job, an innovative joint effort of Tomcat pilot "Heater" Heatley and famed aviation artist Keith Ferris.

from Top Gun — not only the current ACM tricks, but also the gouge on new hardware, changing aspects of missile employment, better briefing and teaching techniques, and the most up-to-date intelligence on known and potential bad guys.

One subject draped in secrecy is the changing capabilities of mid-eighties Soviet aircraft and aviators. Recent unclassified articles by highly regarded Air Force Sovietologist Rana Pennington have cast doubt on long-standing Aggressor and Top Gun doctrine concerning the tactical rigidity and thick-headedness of Russian fighter pilots. The Soviets are known to favor

Soviet MiG-29 Fulcrum shows signs of great aeronautical advancement over previous front-line fighters. It is strange that vision to the rear, poor in most Russian fighters, remains terrible.

large numbers of airplanes precisely controlled and directed by ground commanders. It has long been thought, and taught, that the Russian is an okay flier but an extremely weak aerial tactician, unschooled since birth in anything resembling initiative and hot-seat ingenuity. Teach Ivan some initiative, the old joke goes, and the next thing you know he's flying his Foxbat to Japan.

107

It's a tough quandary for the Soviets. How do you suddenly teach a thirty-year-old, regardless of profession, to think for himself? Might the Communists be leaning toward dissimilar air combat training—Top Guns and Red Flags on the steppes? We've certainly made no secret of these schools and exercises, even inviting Hollywood in on the act. The official word is mum on modern Soviet ACM training—more counting of the holes in the ceiling tile—but one can bet that it has at the very least occurred to them. The Soviets' most recent experience with their current tactical doctrine, the Bekaa Valley Turkey Shoot, can have

hardly increased their confidence. Although most of the unfortunate pilots were Syrian, the airplanes, the training, ground control, surface-to-air threats, and the tactics were all Russian. It's hard to imagine how the results (eighty-two Israeli air-to-air victories without a single Syrian win) could have been worse. Soviet military heads are known to have rolled—literally.

Flat-black Top Gun F-5, decked out for the movie, sports Cyrillic personalization.

The new generation of Soviet fighters will certainly change the balance somewhat. An impressive sextet of MiG-29 Fulcrums recently made a guest appearance at a Finnish air show, and western photographers were able to commit them to razor-sharp Kodachrome for a change. The fighter looks, not surprisingly, like a hybrid of the F-15 and F-18, with twin tails, a modern semi-cranked wing, and the usual huge engines. Espionage undoubtedly has played a part in its mimicry of Western design, but modern aerodynamic logic dictates certain universal realities, spies or no spies. The Fulcrum even sports some interesting features worthy of our attention such as its huge crop-duster tires for soft-field operation and a clever pair of dorsal engine intakes that permit the main inlets to be closed for FOD (foreign object damage) protection when the jet lands in the rough. To the delight of western ACM experts, the single-seat MiG-29 is still burdened with a common Soviet design flaw—lousy vision to the rear. Better check six, Ivan.

Like their NATO teen-fighter counterparts, the Russian RAM-jets are no doubt easier to fly than the Floggers and Fishbeds they supplement (note I didn't use the word "replace"—the Russians seem only to add new planes, never to retire old ones). This factor alone will help the Warsaw Pact pilots make a better ACM showing. The fighters are also thought to be mounted with pretty good digital radars that may make their pilots less dependent on ground commanders and controllers for the intercept.

Top Gun academicians are careful not to spend too much time and attention on Soviet fighter pilots, jets and tactics; despite the spectacle of Maverick and Iceman somehow coming across a Russian five-ship in the middle of the Indian Ocean, the likelihood of U.S. naval aviators shooting at elements of Soviet Frontal Aviation is, thankfully, very remote. The vast majority of Soviet military aircraft are locked to land bases in Russia and Eastern Europe. Despite the enor-

Fly-by-wire Mirage 2000 is a top-flight '80s fighter being sold by the French throughout the Middle East.

mous growth of a huge and very flashy Soviet surface navy, the fleets are almost totally without blue-water air assets as soon as they journey more than a few hundred miles from their shores. The few Soviet aircraft carriers are really antisubmarine vessels, much like the British mini-carriers that almost wound up terminally over their heads in the South Atlantic. Their tiny flight decks can only handle helos and vertical-takeoff jets; the lone Russian naval fighter, the YAK-36 Forger, is an utterly indifferent VSTOL hummer that can scarcely stay out of its own way. Interestingly, the Communists are known to be building one and possibly two American-style supercarriers for the first time in their history, and they probably plan to operate navalized Floggers and RAM-jets from these full-size decks. Not to worry, however. As an American flattop skipper told me several years ago, "It took us half a century to learn how to operate this thing tactically without killing ourselves. How long do you think it's going to take them?"

Of far more immediate concern, at Top Gun and the U.S.A.F. fighter think tanks, are the scores of air forces around the globe that might be potential adversaries. As the Brits found out to their dismay, bloody fights can crop up in the strangest places. Countries throughout the Middle East are all too well-stocked with modern aerial hardware—Soviet, French, British, Swedish, even, God help us, American. The late, lamented Shah of Iran bought eighty Tomcats with early model Phoenix missiles, right off the Grumman line; current intelligence and eyewitness reports indicate that few if any are operational due to the lack of U.S. maintenance and parts support. Phantoms abound, and the Saudis have F-15s and E-3 AWACS with current software. The French, bless their hearts, have sold Mirages to all sorts of less-than-savory types that we turned away.

Other potential battles loom all over the world. Korea could easily heat up at any time. Thailand and the Philippines are in political and military flux. In Central America several countries are involved in ongoing insurgencies. Mexico is a political and economic shambles; many perspicacious observers think it, rather than the less significant countries to the south, is the ultimate Soviet target in the region (the largest KGB headquarters in the world, outside of Moscow, is in Mexico City). Cuba operates Russian-built fighters one hundred miles from NAS Key West, Florida.

And it's mighty convenient that American adversary outfits lean almost exclusively on the A-4 and F-5; more than 40 countries around the world fly one or both of these types, and some are a lot less than friendly. A tidy little air force of Tigers was left behind in Vietnam, and the Communists appear to be putting the reliable little jets to good use. A handful of F-5s was spared this pitiful fate when some enterprising Navy types shanghaied a couple of Air Force HH-3 "Green Giant" rescue helos and sling-lifted the Tigers onto the carrier *Midway* in the closing days of the bugout. At least two jets got dropped into the water in the process, but all involved in this escapade were in agreement that that was preferable to leaving them on the beach. These birds became the first of the Top Gun Tiger fleet, a fate certainly preferable to winding up as *real* Aggressors.

Much has been made of the Top Gun instructors emulating Russian aerial tactics. There is an element of confusion here—this is the game of the Air Force Aggressor squadrons, and even they

Top Gun's F-5F #50 carries Swedish Viggen zigzag camouflage.

are becoming less parochial in their threat simulations. Those camouflage schemes, a different paint job on each Top Gun fighter, aren't all representative of the Warsaw Pact; one is a Libyan paint scheme, another Vietnamese, and one F-5 two-seater even sports a strange zig-zag pattern sprayed onto the Swedish Viggen. Top Gun does simulate the performance characteristics of Soviet fighters, especially the ubiquitous MiG-17 and MiG-21, but in most of the Power Projection ACM engagements the Top Gun teachers are fly-ing a whole lot smarter than the typical Communist trainee. While some Soviet air doctrine does enter into the picture, particularly in the lots-of-bogeys fights, the overriding principle at Top Gun is to fly the simulators as well and innovatively as possible. A Navy pilot who can defeat a Top Gun teacher simulating a Fishbed should be able to take out any Fishbed driver on the planet, regardless of his training, experience, ideology, or whatever. This is also the methodology of the Israeli Air Force, whom the Navy jocks consider the second-best aerial tacticians in the world— after themselves, of course. Train to beat the best flier in the sky, say the Israelis, and then go out and fight as you train.

In a sense it's a shame the world's Top Guns can't get together more often to compare notes. Top Gun teachers make guest appearances at friendly air force bases around the world, although their increasingly tight schedule has cut down on this sort of exchange. Visiting foreign pilots do stop by Hangar One, especially if a nearby Red Flag exercise has invited, say, Cana-

dian or NATO participation. There has even been a bit of intercourse with the vaunted Israelis over the years, although they have an annoying tendency not to be very forthcoming with the juicy details of their combat experiences.

In fact, any American pilot would love a face-to-face with one of his Commie counterparts—no politics or name-calling, just one fighter driver to another. The Navy pilots at Miramar live and breathe flying, and there's no reason to expect the best of the Motherland's flying forces to be any different. I can see it now—drag Ivan into the Miramar Officer's Club bar at quitting time, pass around a few shooters of Stolichnaya, and those knife-edge hands would be shooting each other down in no time.

Just keep the comrade out of the club on Wednesday night or we'll be talking defection city. Most naval installations open the club one night a week to guests of the opposite sex; at Oceana and Pearl it's Friday, and at Miramar it's Big Wednesday. The pilots start drifting in around five o'clock; flight suits are de rigueur, with some pilots yanking off their Velcro name tags and switching to the unofficial call-sign versions. Top Gun staffers prefer to stick with their unique brown leather tags. Pilots from other bases concoct various ruses to "RON" (remain overnight) with their jets; just last week I overheard a Marine Phantom back-seater phoning home to say that the poor old Rhino had broken down and, try as they might, he and his pilot just weren't going to make it home until Thursday. Sure, boys. There's plenty of time for a bit of hero-pilot talk ("there I was, pipes lit, flat on my back at 30,000 feet") before the deejay shows up, legions of girls not far behind. By 9 P.M. the two bars and the huge outside patio are jammed with preening jet jocks

Top Gun staff's lone Air Force instructor stands out during full-dress change of command ceremony for incoming skipper Comdr. Rick "Wigs" Ludwig.

and literally hundreds of spectacular California sweethearts. It's been a popular San Diego institution for years, but since the release of the film *Top Gun* things have gotten completely out of hand. One doesn't hear the boys complaining, however.

One memorable Wednesday night, during the filming of the movie, practically the entire cast and crew dropped by to see what all the fuss was about. They were tricked out and blow-dried to the Hollywood max, but they might as well have been transparent. The girls come to Wednesday Night looking for fighter pilots, not mere movie types. The normally affable Tom Cruise, among others, was a tad miffed at having picked the wrong profession.

Amazingly, even though surrounded by pulchritudinous party animals, many of the Wednesday Night flyboys just keep talking airplanes as if they were still in the ready room. Flying is their existence; everything else gets ranked from number two on down. Says a Tomcat

Fighter pilots love their hot cars, with rear-engine Porsches leading the most-desirable list.

XO, "The Navy gives me this neat $30 million toy, gives me a $3 billion boat to land it on, fills me up with gas, and on top of that they pay me!" I've heard it a hundred times: flying a fighter is the greatest thing this side of sex. Lots of pilots don't even make that qualification.

Nonflying Navy types bitch about the boys-and-their-toys syndrome, and they're right. The fighter mentality extends to the realm of ground transport as well. The fighter and attack types are heavily into hot wheels—Corvettes, Mazda RX-7s, Toyota MR-2s (a rising favorite) and, above all, the Porsche 911. Forget the front-engine 944s and 928s; fighter jocks crave the cantankerous, hard-to-handle rear-engine Porsches. The Navy's reenlistment bonus for carrier pilots can climb as high as $36,000, just about enough (coincidentally?) to snap up a new red 911SC from the not-so-dumb Porsche dealer across from Miramar's north gate.

Retention of Navy pilots is a serious problem, as the bonus program indicates. The boys love the flying, and these days the money isn't half bad. The bugaboo is the cruise—eight months and more on the boat, living like a monk (or a prisoner, according to some), completely isolated from home and family. It's exciting the first time around, especially with stopovers at favorite liberty ports like Perth and Majorca. The second time it's a whole lot less fun. By the time the third one looms, the pilot might well be thinking about changing his way of living, particularly if he's a family man who's had his kids complete whole school grades without him around. Wife and kids are lobbying for dad to fly something else, perhaps a 727 or a corporate Learjet. Other friends who've recently gone civilian keep chiming in with the same idea. You've done more than

enough for the Navy and your country, they say. It's time to live a little! Make big dough! Spend some time at home for a change!

The problem is nearly impossible to solve. The bonuses are a step in the right direction; the Navy certainly doesn't mind spending $36,000 if it can thereby keep for another few years a man it has spent over $1 million to train. Even more valuable is the man's experience as an operational pilot and a squadron officer. If the aviator can be helped over the hump of restlessness and disillusionment that seems to manifest itself between his ninth and twelfth years, the Navy stands a good chance of keeping him for the full twenty years that make him eligible for retirement.

In addition, carrier cruises are being shortened somewhat, but a crisis somewhere in the world can extend a cruise by several months. This is a

Top Gun film crews shot actual dogfights from mountain peaks at NAS Fallon, Nevada. Ops officer Bob "Rat" Willard (*center without shirt*) choreographs dogfights by radio.

dreaded but almost commonplace development. The Navy has periodically toyed with the idea of staffing carrier battle groups with double crews, as it does with its nuclear submarines, but the cost would be horrendous.

The fighter driver who does go civilian risks the agonies of fighter withdrawal. Bussing passengers around in a 727, or waiting at a small airport for the boss to return to the corporate jet, just doesn't cut it. It's flying, sure, but . . . Fighter jocks have trouble shaking off the need for speed. The perfect solution for a limited number is the Naval Reserve. Under the Total Force concept supported so enthusiastically by SecNav Lehman (who flies Reserve helos and also serves as a bombardier-navigator in an A-6 Intruder), Reservists get to fly the most current Navy equipment, including the Tomcat, the Hornet, the E-2C Hawkeye, the A-6 heavy bomber, and more. Talk about the best of both worlds. Not surprisingly, Reserve slots are hard to come by. Some highly regarded pilots, like *Fighter Combat* author and former Top Gun instructor Bob Shaw, have managed to wheedle interservice transfers to Air Force Reserve and Air National Guard outfits flying F-4s, F-15s, F-16s and other exotic hardware.

For those Fleet and Marine pilots who remain at the tip of naval aviation's sword, faced with the ever-present possibility of meeting vastly superior enemy numbers in aerial combat, Top Gun will continue to serve as the fountainhead of ACM wisdom and doctrine. But before and after Top Gun, one problem remains for the squadrons—in the aerial arena, there is no substitute for practice. Dogfighting is a razor-edge skill, and luminaries like Duke Cunningham (currently the skipper of West Coast adversaries), have publicly expressed

concern that Fleet fighter pilots aren't getting nearly enough ACM experience. The dual-role F-18 is a hell of a dogfighter, but a large number of its Navy pilots, having come to the Hornet from the light-attack A-7 world, have had all too little ACM experience. Top Gun has its work cut out for it. In the Vietnam debacle, Navy fighter pilots were presented with a timely gift: a four-year air war hiatus in which they could pull their collective act together and relearn lessons all too easily forgotten. In the next aerial tussle—be it in the southern Mediterranean, off the coast of Southeast Asia, or high above units of the Red Banner Fleet—it's going to have to be done right the first time. As they say at Top Gun, no points for second place.

Only the Spirit of attack, born in a brave heart will bring success to any fighter aircraft no matter how highly developed it may be

GALLAND

Glossary

AAA Antiaircraft Artillery. Rapid-firing cannon or machine guns, often aimed by computers and radar.

ACM Air Combat Maneuvering, or dogfighting.

AGL An airplane's altimeter reads height above Mean Sea Level (MSL); the more realistic measurement over land is height Above Ground Level.

Air Wing The entire complement of aircraft fielded by the carrier in battle: fighters, attack jets, early-warning planes, tankers, helicopters, antisubmarine patrol craft, etc.

Angle of Attack Angle of the wing relative to the forward flight path of the airplane. On any aircraft, too great an angle of attack will cause the wing to stop flying, as airflow across the upper surface is cut off.

Angles Gaining angles on a dogfight opponent involves maneuvering for a shot from astern. The ultimate in an angles fight is an angle of zero—straight behind the enemy's tailpipe.

ASW Antisubmarine warfare.

Atoll, Apex, Acrid NATO code names for Soviet-manufactured air-to-air missiles.

Bag Flight suit.

Ball The primary optical landing device on the carrier deck.

Bandit Dogfight adversary positively identified as a bad guy.

Bat-Turn A tight, high-G change of heading. A reference to the rapid 180-degree Batmobile maneuver in the old "Batman" television series.

Bingo Minimum fuel for a comfortable and safe return to base. Aircraft can fly and fight past bingo fuel in combat situations, but at considerable peril.

Bingo Field Land runway to which carrier craft can divert if necessary.

Blue-Water Ops Carrier flight operations beyond the reach of land bases or bingo fields.

Bogey Unidentified and potentially hostile aircraft.

Bolt, Bolter A carrier landing attempt in which the hook fails to engage any of the arresting wires.

Bounce, Tap Unexpected attack on another aircraft.

Burner Afterburner; a system that feeds raw fuel into a jet's hot exhaust, thus greatly increasing both thrust and fuel consumption.

CAG Commander of the Air Group—the carrier's chief pilot.

Carqual Carrier qualification; a set number of carrier takeoffs and landings required in training and at periodic intervals of all carrier flight crews.

Cat Shot A carrier takeoff assisted by a steam-powered catapult. A "cold cat," one in which insufficient launch pressure has been set into the device, can place the hapless aircraft in the water. A "hot cat"—too much pressure—is less perilous, but can rip out the nose wheel assembly or the launching bridle. Once a pair of common problems, but practically unheard-of today.

Check Six Visual observation of the rear quadrant, from which most air-to-air attacks can be expected. Refers to the clock system of scanning the envelope around the aircraft: 12 o'clock is straight ahead, 6 o'clock is dead aft. Also a common salutation and greeting among tactical pilots.

COD Carrier On-Board Delivery aircraft, used to transfer personnel and cargo to and from the carrier deck.

Contract Agreements and ground rules, some minor and some life-threatening, between two-man fighter crews or between wingmen.

Dash Two The second plane in a two-ship formation; the wingman.

Departure Literally departure from controlled flight; usually brought on in high-performance jets by excessive angle of attack coupled with partial power loss in one engine. All aircraft depart differently, but some anxious moments and some loss of altitude will result before control can be regained. Some jets, most notably the F-4 Phantom, are unrecoverable from certain departures.

Double Nuts The CAG's bird, usually numbered 100 or 00.

Double Ugly Fond nickname for the enormously capable but less than beautiful F-4 Phantom. See also Rhino.

Echo Range A corner of the China Lake Naval Weapons Test Center outfitted with ground targets and electronic threat simulators. Many Top Gun training sessions are flown over Echo Range.

ECM Electronic Countermeasures; systems for jamming or misleading enemy weapons, communications, and radar.

Electric Jet The F-16 Fighting Falcon, so nicknamed because of its fly-by-wire controls.

ELINT Electronic Intelligence; the gathering of electronic emissions related to communications, weapons control, or reconnaissance.

Envelope An aircraft's operational parameters.

FARP Fleet ACM Readiness Program; a periodic training program presented in the context of the Fleet Air Wing.

FASO Flight Physiology Training; recurrent safety training for naval aircrews.

FAST Fleet Air Superiority Training.

Fishbed, Flogger Also Fitter, Flanker, Fresco, Fulcrum, etc. NATO code names for Soviet fighter aircraft.

Flare The nose-up landing posture normal for most land-based aircraft. Carrier jets eliminate flare in favor of a slamming contact with the deck.

Fly-by-wire Electronic, computer-controlled operation of aircraft control surfaces. Supplants mechanical/hydraulic actuation common in earlier jets. The F-16, F-18, and the French Mirage 2000 use these systems.

FOD Foreign Object Damage. A constant concern on airfields and carrier decks where jet engines operate. Jet intakes can ingest loose objects, and even the smallest item—a rock, a bolt—can seriously damage jet turbine blades.

Fox One, Two, Three Radio calls indicating the firing of a Sparrow, Sidewinder, or Phoenix air-to-air missile, respectively.

Furball A confused aerial engagement with many combatants.

G, G-loading, G-rating High-performance aircraft subject airframes and occupants to centrifugal forces far beyond simple gravity. One-G equals normal gravity; a pilot and plane pulling 4-Gs in a turn will feel the forces equal to four times the weight of gravity.

G-suit Nylon trousers that wrap around the legs and abdomen. Filled automatically with compressed air in high-G maneuvers, the G-suit helps prevent the pooling of blood in the lower extremities, thus retarding the tendency to lose consciousness.

Glove The huge wing root of the F-14 Tomcat, housing the mechanism for moving the variable-geometry wings. Also, Tom Cruise notwithstanding, fireproof gloves are always worn by combat pilots despite the heat.

Gomer Slang for a dogfight adversary, the usage presumably stemming from the old Gomer Pyle television show.

Gouge The latest inside information. Also the poop, the skinny.

Hard Deck An established minimum altitude for training engagements. Early Top Gun hops honor a 10,000-foot AGL hard deck.

Helo Universal Navy/Marine term for helicopter. Don't say "chopper" unless you're hanging out with the Army.

HOTAS Hands On Throttle And Stick. Modern fighters have every imaginable control function

mounted on either the stick (right hand) or the throttle quadrant (left hand), so that the pilot need not fumble around in the cockpit.

HUD Head Up Display. A transparent screen mounted on the dashboard, on which pertinent data from flight instruments and weapons systems are projected. The HUD eliminates the need to look down into the cockpit to read instruments.

Hummer Any ingenious machine—plane, car, weapon—whose actual name can't be recalled. Also "puppy," "bad boy." The E-2 Hawkeye early-warning aircraft is also nicknamed the Hummer, in reference to the sound of its turbo-prop engines.

IFR Instrument Flight Rules, permitting safe flight in conditions of limited visibility.

INS Inertial Navigation System. A device that,

properly loaded and aligned, permits the pilot to determine his location anywhere on earth within a few hundred feet.

Jock, Driver Pilot.

Knife Fight Close-in low-speed aerial dogfight.

Lethal Cone, Cone of Vulnerability Area to the rear of the jet's tailpipe, into which most infrared missile and gun attacks are ideally launched.

Loading/Unloading Increasing or decreasing angle of attack and Gs.

Loud Handle Lever or grip that fires ejection seat.

LSO Landing Signal Officer. Squadron member with considerable experience in carrier landings, responsible for assisting others onto the deck and for grading their efforts.

Merge, Merged Plot The point at which aircraft come into contact, after having been vectored toward each other by radar control.

MiGCAP Combat Air Patrol over ground-attack aircraft.

Military Power Maximum jet engine power without engaging afterburner.

Mud-mover, Ground-pounder Low-level attack aircraft such as the A-6 and A-7. The F/A-18 doubles as a fighter and a mud-mover.

NATOPS The Naval Aviation Training and Operations Directorate, responsible for rules and regulations governing the safe and correct operation of all naval aircraft.

NFWS The Navy Fighter Weapons School, a graduate school for fighter pilots. Its universal nickname is Top Gun.

No Joy Failure to make visual sighting.

Nylon Letdown Ejection.

OAST Overland Air Superiority Training. A periodic training exercise conducted over land and integrating all the elements of the carrier's air wing.

Pass The point at which fighters, closing head-on, flash past each other.

Pit Rear seat position of the F-14 Tomcat or F-4 Phantom.

Pole Control stick.

Radome Streamlined fiberglass enclosure covering a radar antenna.

RAG Replacement Air Group. Squadron in which newly trained pilots are introduced to and trained in a particular aircraft type.

Red Flag A large mock air war, held quarterly by the Air Force at Nellis AFB, Nevada. Many non–Air Force assets—Navy/Marines, Army, foreign—are invited to participate.

Rhino Nickname for the F-4 Phantom. See Double Ugly.

RIO Radar Intercept Officer. Back-seat crewman in the F-14 and F-4.

SA Situational Awareness. An all-encompassing term for keeping track of what's happening when flying a high-performance aircraft at its limits. SA involves knowing what your airplane is doing relative to its envelope, where your adversary is and what he's up to, where the ground is, the status of enemy threats on the ground, and a hundred other factors.

SAM Surface-to-air missile.

Scooter Nickname for the A-4 Skyhawk, used as a MiG simulator at Top Gun.

Sierra Hotel Polite phonetics for "shit hot," the fighter pilot's favorite and all-purpose expression of approval.

Speed Jeans G-suit.

Speed of Heat, Warp One Very, very fast.

TACAN Navigation aid giving bearing and distance between an airplane and the ground or aircraft carrier.

TACTS Tactical Aircrew Combat Training System. A system of computers, sensors, data pods, and graphic displays that permits real-time depiction of an aerial dogfight. TACTS is an integral element of Top Gun training.

Three-Nine Line Imaginary line across your airplane's wings. A primary goal in ACM is to keep your adversary in front of your three-nine line.

Tits Machine A good, righteous airplane. Current airplanes need not apply; this is a nostalgic term referring to birds gone by. By all accounts the F-8 Crusader was a tits machine.

Tits-up Broken, not functioning.

Trap Arrested aircraft carrier landing.

Turkey Nickname for the F-14 Tomcat.

VSTOL Vertical or Short Takeoff and Landing. The AV-8 Harrier is a VSTOL aircraft, capable of vectoring its jet thrust to shorten its takeoff roll or even to rise and descend vertically.

Warthog Universal nickname for the A-10 Thunderbolt II close air support aircraft.

Whiskey Delta Phonetics for "weak dick," a pilot who can't cut it. Such a scurrilous term that it's almost never used.

Wingman Second pilot in a two-ship pair, responsible for ensuring that his leader's six o'clock remains clear.

The Author and Photographer

Geoge Hall is a San Francisco photographer and writer specializing in aerial and aviation topics. His photographs illustrate other Presidio AIRPOWER books, including CV: CARRIER AVIATION, USAFE: A PRIMER OF MODERN AIR COMBAT IN EUROPE, RED FLAG: AIR COMBAT FOR THE '80s, and MARINE AIR: FIRST TO FIGHT, and are also featured in the annual AIRPOWER Calendar.